HEARING GOD & SLAYING
GIANTS
IN
YOUR CAREER

It's Not About You Working.
It's About God Working In You.

by
Darryl Brumfield

Hearing God & Slaying Giants in Your Career

Copyright ©2016 by Darryl Brumfield

ISBN: 978-1-48356-205-6

Unless otherwise indicated, Scripture quotations in this book at taken from the New King James Version of the Bible. Copyright © 1979, 1980, 1984 by Thomas Nelson, Inc., Publishers.

The Holy Bible, New International Version®, NIV® Copyright © 1973, 1978, 1984, 2011 by Biblica, Inc.® Used by permission. All rights reserved worldwide.

Cover and interior design by Steve Shultz

Printed in the United States of America.

Contents

Acknowledgements

I would like to express my appreciation to the people who help me publish this book. By God's grace, each of you provided what I needed when I needed it.

I would like to thank my wife Linda for her support. You have been amazing. In spite of the time that this project took me away from you, you have always been my biggest cheerleader. It's a blessing when your wife is also your best friend. I love you.

I would like to thank my mom, El Marie, and my family. God used all of you to mold me into the person I am today. Mom (McFaw), you are a woman of God who lives out your faith with both wisdom and zeal. You and dad raised us in an atmosphere of love with a sense of purpose and destiny. Thanks for being a role model and providing a great foundation for all of us. Beverly (Bev), I bet you a dollar to a donut that no one has a big sister like you. Thanks for everything. Lois (Lo), Murchelle (Skoker!), Murray (Brum), Gary (Gay) and Vinnie, I love and appreciate all of you. And finally Dad (Papa), it's been more than 10 years since you went home to be with the Lord. I still miss you. To be a man you have to see a man; I saw you and I am the better for it.

I would like to thank my children. Darryl Jr (Tike) and Marie (Princess) you have had a front row seat to many of the ups and downs that I wrote about. It was my love and commitment to the both of you that pushed me to not give up on God during the most turbulent years of my life. In spite of my occasional lapses in faith, I always felt your unconditional love and support. Taliyah (TaTa), Nicole (NikNik) and Melieck, I see wonderful bits and pieces of your Mom in each of you, but I also see your own God-given greatness in all its colors. I hope this book motivates each of you to never give up on your dreams.

I want to thank my friends. I have been blessed with some great friendships; friends that are like family. In closing, I want to single out Dave Gibbons, Michelle Jones and Steve Shultz, three friends that God used to help me publish the my story. Dave, through many conversations you convinced me that this book was the one that I should write. Michelle (MJ) thanks for blessing me with your amazing gift of communication. Your input and counsel helped me tell my story with clarity. Steve I can't express how much I appreciate the time you put into this project. Thanks for your editing, proofreading and artwork.

Forward

Principles for living frequently can be learned best by looking at models, and Darryl Brumfield provides a great model to see how God can work in a life.

By intertwining his own testimony with the recounting of the life of the David of the Bible, Darryl is able to provide both a biblical and a personal basis for laying out foundational principles for living.

Sometimes Christians give the impression that the abundant life in Jesus Christ brings a smooth upward journey. But life is not always upward. We live in a fallen world. We can grow as we learn to cultivate an overcoming spirit in difficult times. Success may be learning how to cope with hard times as well as achieving in good times.

Darryl Brumfield's story provides a discipling tool for both the reader and ones they mentor. It provides a special encouragement to those struggling in their work life.

Carl Westerlund
Pastor, Calvary Chapel Costa Mesa

Introduction

I arrived at the San Jose Airport about five hours before I was scheduled to speak at a weekend retreat. I wanted to take a nap as we made the drive from the airport to the retreat center, but when the young man who was driving me to the retreat center asked, "So Darryl, how did you get into technology?" My nap was abruptly and permanently halted. My answer to his question left him speechless. After a brief pause, looking somewhat dumbfounded, he said, "Wow, that's amazing. So then what happened?" For the next two hours, I explained what happened.

My explanation initiated an emotional roller coaster ride that consumed our three-hour drive. As I unpacked my career in technology, at times, we laughed uncontrollably. But our laughter would always give way to reflection, as we pondered the power and person of God. When we arrived at the retreat center, the young man said, "Darryl, you need to write a book about your story."

Although I share in great detail how God helped me successfully transition from one employer to the next, this book isn't about interview techniques or how to advance in your career. This is not a book about God helping me search for a job, but rather one about GOD HELPING ME FIND HIM AS I SEARCHED FOR A JOB.

Seriously, it's not like God needs to help us find work, ever. If he wants us working tomorrow, can he not make that happen with a little more than a thought? Whatever your employment status, know that what God is doing in your life right now is bigger than a mere job.

The title and cover of this book are intended to remind the reader of the classic story of "David and Goliath" with our contemporary challenges in both career and life. Regardless of one's religious affiliation or belief, most people can relate to the story of David and Goliath. Like David, most people have faced a giant at some point in their life. A medical opinion, relationship conflict or a depressing economic forecast can become menacing giants that taunt us like Goliath taunted David. Unfortunately, most of us don't face our giants the same way that David faced his.

It seems that with every job change, I had to face a giant. Most of the time, the giants were in my head. I created them by factoring God out of the equation. The faith that David displayed was often absent in my situation. Maybe that's where you are today.

If you or someone you know has allowed a bleak economic outlook or unemployment statistics to fill your heart with fear and distort your view of God, this book may help you pause and begin to see that God is bigger than your current unemployment or financial crisis. God is still in charge. God still reigns, and God is still in the business of helping Davids slay Goliaths.

CHAPTER 1

The Lion, the Bear & the Giraffe

David said to Saul, "Your servant has been keeping his father's sheep. When a lion or a bear came and carried off a sheep from the flock, I went after it struck it and rescued the sheep from its mouth. When it turned on me, I seized it by its hair, struck it and killed it." [1]

We are not born with an innate desire to trust God; trusting God is the byproduct of experiencing God's favor, time and time again. Developing and nurturing a healthy confidence and expectation in God is much like developing trust toward a biological parent.

[1] 1 Samuel 17:34-35

The first time a child leaps from the edge of the pool into the water, they are extremely tentative. Before they have enough confidence to take that first leap, they often need a lot of coaching and encouragement. Over time, they jump into the water without any reservations. The timidity and fear that marked that first leap is replaced with laughter because the child knows, through experience, that their loving parent would not allow them to drown.

In David's eyes, God was more than an abstract deity who cherished animal sacrifices and religious rituals. For David, God was a real person who was with him at work. His encounters with a lion and a bear shaped David's view of God at an early age.[2] When the lion came, David leaped into God's arms and when the bear came, David took another leap.

I'm guessing that the second leap was easier than the first. But one thing I can say with a measure of certainty, as a shepherd boy, David learned that God could be trusted. Like David, as a young boy, I

[2] 1 Samuel 17:36

discovered that God is more than capable of catching us, if we would only take that leap of faith.

In my formative years, I wasn't a great student. I didn't excel in academics in high school, middle school, or elementary school. In fact, if not for a very persistent Pentecostal mom, I would have fallen through the cracks of the public education system. To make sure I received more than a remedial education, my mother went to bat for me on several occasions. When I was in the second grade, she took her first swing.

As a second grader, I had a very noticeable speech impediment. Because kids can be very cruel in elementary school, I dreaded reading in public. Whenever it was my turn to read in class, the following ritual would take place. Before I uttered one word, the palms of my hands would sweat, then my brow, and within a short time, I would be drenched in perspiration. As I struggled to pronounce the words in front of me, I would hear a chorus of subdued laughter followed by the teacher's plea for civility.

One day I decided to change the script, so with all the wisdom that a second grader could muster, I came up with an ingenious plan. I would sabotage reading time. For several weeks I did everything I could do to disrupt the class. However, one morning, I crossed the line. While no one was looking, I booby trapped the room. I placed tacks in some of my classmates' chairs, and I put chalk in the chairs of others. As planned, my antics created the distraction that I desired. My teacher was forced to abruptly shut down reading time.

My past behavior, coupled with the fact that my hands were covered with chalk made me the prime suspect for the "chalk-tack-gate" conspiracy. After a brisk heated interrogation, I confessed to the crime. My confession, however, did not placate my teacher. She had tried the usual disciplinary action with me and was looking for an alternative.

They had special classes for kids like me. My teacher thought it was time that I joined the other disruptive kids that were not keeping up. In an attempt to remove me from her class and mainstream education altogether, she scheduled a parent conference.

When my mom showed up to the school for the parent conference to decide my fate, she was calm but defiant. When the conference started, my teacher began to make her case. "Mrs. Brumfield, Darryl is causing problems." "Mrs. Brumfield, Darryl doesn't pay attention." "Mrs. Brumfield, Darryl does this, and Mrs. Brumfield, Darryl doesn't do that."

To be perfectly honest, I was hoping that my mom wouldn't fight for me. I wasn't excelling, and I was looking for an easy way out. Joining a classroom where I wouldn't be forced to read in public seemed like an appealing remedy, but, my mom wasn't the least bit swayed by my teacher and the other school representatives. She politely told them what they could do with their class, then gave them some assurance that my behavior would change.

When we returned home, my mom and I had a heart-to-heart talk. She knew that my speech was playing a factor in my destructive behavior, so she addressed it head on. She went to the cupboard and reached for her bottle of olive oil.

Now, my mom knew that there wasn't power in the oil, but she believed that God, who is all powerful, could work through the olive oil. On many occasions before and after this chapter in my life, my mother would anoint me with olive oil and pray. I was a sickly kid, so my mom went through a lot of olive oil.

Holding the olive oil firmly in her right hand, she said, "Darryl, do you believe that God can loosen your tongue?" I replied, "Yes, I believe." My mom then took the oil and rubbed it on my lips and said, "Lord, we believe that you can loosen his tongue." Then over the duration of her prayer, beginning with the time I almost died as a toddler, she recounted many of the times that God intervened in my life.

After concluding her prayer, she said, "Now your lips belong to God, but your butt belongs to me, so this is the end of acting up in school. You have to believe God; you have to trust Him for yourself. I can't do that part for you." I nodded, and took her words to heart.

The next day, I faced my giant. It was time to read and, as was our custom, each kid read a few sentences from our book. I remember counting the kids that were in front of me in the reading order. Based on my calculations, I would have to read a very difficult passage, a passage that included my most dreaded word:

giraffe. If you promised me the world, I could not pronounce the word giraffe.

When I was on deck, my heart was pounding and I imagined hearing the snickering of my classmates. In my mind, I saw myself struggling to read the few sentences that were in front of me. But a strange thing happened. This time, when my palms began to sweat, I remembered my mom's words, "You have to believe for yourself. I can't do that part for you." Then, without much thought, I took a leap of faith and faced my giant words that were in front of me. To my amazement, the words seemed to roll off my tongue, including the word giraffe.

After school, I ran all the way home and along the way I periodically shouted out, Giraffe! Giraffe! Giraffe! When I arrived at home, I found my mom in the kitchen. After I told her the good news, we had a praise party. My mom broke into dance and blurted out a few Hallelujahs.

That day was one of the happiest days of my life. Moreover, it remains one of the most important days of my life. As a second grader, I learned that miracles do happen, and that by God's grace, you can slay giants.

What I learned in the second grade prepared me for the rest of my life and underpins every job story in this book.

Faith, like a seed, must be sown and nurtured before it can produce fruit. God used the paw of the Lion and the paw of the Bear to plant and nurture David's faith. Before David stepped up to face Goliath in the public square, he first faced lesser foes in obscurity.

God doesn't just throw you out to fight giants without providing the necessary preparation. Like a well-managed, promising prize fighter, God hand-picks your opponents. He literally sets them up so that you can knock them down.

In the second grade I faced a giant named Giraffe. And by God's grace, I took a leap of faith and knocked it down. In doing that, I learned that you can sweat and still have faith. I learned that faith doesn't immediately remove all of your insecurities. Most of all, I learned that God shows up when we take a leap of faith. When we listen to the still small voice that is telling us to go for it in spite of our past failures, we can slay giants.

God wants you to succeed and, if you think about it, he has been prepping you for success. Have you forgotten past victories? If so, take some time to meditate on how God helped you in the past. He did not help you in the past to abandon you in the present.

God is still intimately engaged in every aspect of your life using trials to both develop your character and draw you closer to him. So now is not the time to give up; it's time to remember what God has done, and believe that he is more than capable of doing that and more now. As you will see, beginning with the next chapter, whenever we take a leap of faith and face our giant, we give God an opportunity to show up and do more than we could ever ask or even think.

CHAPTER 2

The Darryl Brumfield Story

"The LORD who rescued me from the paw of the Lion and the paw of the Bear will rescue me from the hand of this Philistine."[3]

After my encounter with God as a second grader, my pronunciation skills improved significantly; however, my ability to pay attention in class remained a problem. Many years later, as an adult, I discovered that I had Attention Deficit Disorder (ADD). Due in part to ADD, from grade school to high school, at best, I was a mediocre student. In fact, in the seventh and tenth grades I was placed in remedial classes. However, each time I was removed from the college prep track, my mom

---

[3] 1 Samuel 17:37

scheduled a parent conference and forced the school to reverse the remedial curriculum that was assigned to me.

Although I was never more than a C student, the possibility of going to college became a reality for me in 1977 when my brother was accepted into the University of California, at Irvine (UCI). Motivated by my brother's admission into UCI, I improved my academic standing. It wasn't easy. After struggling through the first quarter of my senior year in high school, I met the minimum admissions requirements for UCI by a hair. This did not guarantee a seat at the table, but the accomplishment presented an open door. So, against the odds, I applied to UCI and to my surprise, I was admitted.

I'll never forget the emotion I experienced while I read my acceptance letter. I re-read it several times. Each time I thanked God for extending to me this great opportunity in spite of my dismal academic track record. I thought about all the times that my mom went to bat for me and how God had just hit the ball out of the park; it was sheer bliss.

My first year at UCI was difficult for me academically, because I still struggled with my attention span. Unlike high school, however, the lectures and notes were readily available for review in college. So I figured out a study regimen that worked for me, and for the first time in my life, I received an academic award. I made the honor roll.

I was filled with optimism. I could see myself graduating from UCI in a few years and heading off to law school. After that, I would become a successful corporate lawyer. I had my eye on the prize, my dreams were in sight, and I was pressing toward them with optimism and zeal. But suddenly everything changed. In the first quarter of my sophomore year, I got married.

Neither I nor my bride had any business getting married at our stages of maturity. We were both teenagers, and we had a lot of growing up to do. Because I lacked wisdom and discernment, I thought I was doing the right thing. My marriage was my effort to align my life with what I thought was God's best plan for me.

My pastor, whom I loved dearly, was an old-school, whooping, hand-over-the-ear preacher. He literally scared the hell out of me with his fire and brimstone messages. One of his favorite messages was titled, "It's better to marry than to burn." Much later in life, I found out that the Bible was referring to burning with passion not burning in hell. I sure could have used a good Bible commentary back then. Cutting to the chase, my marriage was my answer to celibacy. Or to state it another way, I thought that getting married would keep me from burning in hell.

Nevertheless, my pastor saw my commitment to serving God and he nourished it. From time to time, he would ask me to preach to the congregation for about three to five minutes. Initially, I would finish my sermon in half the time that was allotted to me, but after a while, I would go over my time limit. When that happened, he would stand up behind me, pull my coattail and say with the voice of a doting but stern father, "Okay, that's enough young man, you can't tell it all." My pastor's abrupt interruption of my sermon would always spark an encouraging applause mixed with some good-hearted laughter from the congregation.

Although I was not aware of his intentions, my pastor had his eye on me for some time, and he was using my three- and five-minute sermons to prepare me to be a preacher. One day, out of the blue, he stood in front of the congregation and pointed to me. In a very solemn tone, with a voice that had grown raspier year after year from preaching at the top of his lungs, he said, "I believe God has called this young man to preach."

His remarks caught me completely off guard. I can't say that I agreed with him, but what was I to do? He had just announced to the whole congregation in a very dramatic and ceremonious fashion that I was called to preach. Next to my dad, there wasn't another man in the entire world that I revered more than JD Jones, my pastor and spiritual father. Thinking that my preaching would never go beyond my local church in Compton, Calif., I sheepishly accepted the mantel that was laid on me.

When I perform a marriage ceremony today, I usually say something like this, "Marriage is honorable and should not be entered into lightly, but advisedly, soberly, and reverently." Well, I did not follow that advice at my own wedding. I entered into my union hurriedly, foolishly and carelessly. And as a result, in a very short time, I found myself with my back against the wall. My bride was pregnant with our first child, I was facing eviction from my landlord, and I was on academic probation at UCI.

It was at this point, when things were most dire, that I reached out to God for help. I was ready to throw in the towel with both school and my now impending responsibility of fatherhood, but God stepped in before I could do either. His intervention, once again, changed the course of my life.

I remember the events as though they happened yesterday. I was sitting on the edge of my bed perplexed and distressed from the weight of my finances. Simply stated, I was so broke that I couldn't pay attention. In the midst of my despair, I began to reflect on my UCI admissions letter. When I opened that acceptance letter, I remembered saying under my breath, "God has the final say. If God decides to intervene in a situation, he can make a difference." Interestingly enough, the more I thought about God, the smaller my problem became. Armed with a simple trust in God, I began to pray.

At some point, in the middle of my prayer, I decided that God was more than able to give me a job;

moreover, God could provide a job that was in my field of interest. So I decided to call every technology company in the area. If God wanted to open a door, then I would find favor with one of the employers in the Yellow Pages.

I began my conversation with each company the same way, "Hello my name is Darryl Brumfield and I'm looking for an internship in the field of computer science." After striking out with the first six or seven companies, I hit pay dirt.

"Hello, my name is Darryl Brumfield and I'm looking for an internship in computer science." I blurted out in a somewhat enthusiastic yet mechanical manner, like a telemarketer making a cold call. But this time, the woman on the other end said something that really shocked me. She said, and I'm not kidding, "Darryl Brumfield! We have been looking for you! When will you be available?" At that point, I almost dropped the phone. After I quickly regained my composure, I told her that I could come in and meet the hiring manager right away.

I showed up for an interview the next day. I remember putting on my suit and tie and walking into the very upscale lobby. At first the receptionist seemed to be a little cold, but she warmed up when I said, "Hello, my name is Darryl Brumfield, I'm here to interview for an internship." She said, smiling from ear to ear with a bit of a sigh in her voice as she uttered my name, "Darryl, where have you been?"

I remember saying under my breath, "Is this really happening?" There are moments where God's favor just overwhelms you. Sometimes, when the favor of God sweeps you off your feet, you actually feel like an observer in your own experience. That's how I felt when, as a second grader, the word giraffe rolled smoothly off my tongue. And that's how I felt when I took my seat and waited for my interview.

As I waited in the lobby, doubt suddenly began to fill my heart. It's amazing how we can sense God's favor one moment and then, in the very next moment, be filled with fear. Suddenly, I was afraid again. I began to tell myself that I was not qualified for an internship in computer science. After all, although I was now leaning toward a career in computer science, I entered UCI as a criminal justice major and I had only taken one computer science class. Secondly, this company was one of the most well-known and well-respected technology companies in the world. I had good reason to doubt that I would be offered an internship.

Looking to impress the hiring manager with a few buzz words, I tried to remember the few things I gleaned from the only computer science course that I had completed. At the time, my knowledge of computer science was extremely limited. To be honest, I barely knew the difference between a for-loop (computer language command) and a Fruit Loop®. I wrestled with my insecurities for several minutes, then I tossed the pending interview back into God's court.

After being ushered into the hiring manager's office, I took a seat and braced myself for a grueling interview. Amazingly, the hiring manager didn't ask me one computer science question. He asked me about hiking, he asked if I liked to ski, and he asked me if I liked to fish. He didn't ask any computer science questions. Even though I didn't ski, hike, or fish, we hit it off and he offered me an internship with the company.

For three weeks I came to work and for three weeks I stared at the same assignment that I was given on my first day of work. The job was way over my head. I had taken one course in computer science, and now I was asked to write a program to compute and report statistical analysis data for the projects in our department. If they had given me the task of computing the navigational orbit of weather satellites, I would have had the same odds of completing it.

Google didn't exist in 1980, so each day I would write down terms and words that I didn't understand and look up the meanings later that evening. Although I was beginning to pick up the terminology, I wasn't mastering the technology. So when my manager called me into his office Monday morning of week four, I thought I was about to be shown the door.

My manager, looking very puzzled, said these words, "Darryl, I received a very strange phone call." He paused, there was a moment of silence, then he continued and said, "Darryl Brumfield just called me. Who are you?" I replied, "I'm Darryl Brumfield!"

Apparently, they had extended an internship to a college senior majoring in computer science. This intern just happened to be named Darryl Brumfield. He had called to apologize for not showing up for the interview due to an accident. He also informed the company that he would not be interested in a position.

After the question of my identity was settled, my manager had a really good laugh. He said, "Darryl, I have never heard of something like this happening." I then explained to him that, although I was just starting my computer science education, I would love to keep working for the company. His answer was music to my ears. He told me that he thought that I was struggling but that he and the rest of the department really liked me. So he decided that he would keep me as an intern for the rest of the year. My assignment: learn as much as I could about computer science, and that's what I did.

For the rest of the year I came to work and studied computer science and when I got stuck, no problem. I was working at one of the most highly respected technology companies in the world. Consequently, I was surrounded by highly skilled engineers. They wrote programs that controlled satellites and missile systems, and they loved to share their knowledge and expertise with me. When my internship concluded, I was well on my way to a promising career in Information Technology (IT).

That's the "Darryl Brumfield Story," my anthem to God's sovereignty, grace, and sense of humor. But most importantly, this slice of my life is being repeated all over the world as people exercise their faith. This is and can be your story too. It's been said that faith doesn't work until you do. There is a lot of truth in that statement. God will ask us to take active steps to validate our faith. When we do that, when we take a step of faith, we embark on a journey. We never know where that act of faith will lead. But we must take the first step to find out what God has in store for us.

Success or failure, more often than not, is dependent upon our willingness to simply step up with whatever we have (or don't have). In that second grade classroom, when I successfully pronounced the word giraffe, I was drenched in sweat. But rather than cower in defeat as was my pattern, I stepped up and God did the rest. In spite of the odds, I stepped up to go to college. Ready or not, I stepped up to be a husband and a father, which lead me to look for a job in IT. God did the rest.

Like David, we must become less concerned with our own readiness and be confident that God is ready to step in when we are willing to step up. David didn't fear the paw of the lion or the paw of the bear. With that same confidence, a young inexperienced David was willing to step up to a giant while others were gripped by fear. So are you willing to step up? You may not be in a strong position. You may be inexperienced, but it doesn't matter. Sometimes it's not about what we bring to the table; sometimes it's about stepping up to the table.

So what crazy, off-the-wall idea is stirring in your heart? I want to encourage you to pray about taking the first step toward your goal. For me, it was as simple as picking up a phone book and making a few phone calls. That one act of faith changed my life and the next steps that you take in faith may change yours. So don't think about the odds and allow the obstacles to paralyze you. Think about how God helped you defeat your bear, lion, or your giraffe, then, by faith, step up and face your giant.

CHAPTER 3

Why Are You Alone?

David went to Nob, to Ahimelech the priest. Ahimelech trembled when he met him, and asked, "Why are you alone? Why is no one with you?"[4]

Fairy tales often end with the phrase, "…and they lived happily ever after." Well, my life isn't a fairy tale and neither was David's. After God helped David kill the giant, David faced a very prolonged trial at the hands of King Saul.[5] And after my God-orchestrated internship ended, I entered one of the most trying seasons of my life. Like the once favored son of Israel who was reduced to lying to Ahimelech to put food in his stomach and a

[4] 1 Samuel 21:1
[5] 1 Samuel 19:1-2

sword in his hand,[6] I went from working at one of the most prestigious technology companies in the world to working a series of low-paying, unskilled jobs.

But how should we view an apparent shift in God's favor? Does a change in our circumstances signal a demotion from favored son status? Certainly not. We can never lose our favored-son status. Trials only serve to clarify what it means to be favored. Though unwelcomed, the next chapter in my life provided me with the much-needed clarification of what it means to be a favored son.

I had learned a great deal about computer science in my first IT job, and the knowledge I gained really helped me with my computer science classes at UCI. However, when my internship ended, I had a hard time landing another IT position. No matter how hard I tried, I was unable to convince an employer to hire me. And with every unsuccessful attempt to secure an IT position, I began to question my faith.

Initially, after my internship concluded, I was filled with hope and optimism. If lightning could strike

[6] 1 Samuel 21:2-3;6,8

once, then it could certainly strike twice. Consistent with my previous employment search, I picked up the Yellow Pages and began to call every large technology company in the area. When that approach failed, I hit the pavement and made personal visits to the large technology companies in the area. When that failed, I religiously poured through the classifieds on a daily basis, without any success.

Still, I was not deterred. I had been on a roll, and I was certain that my faith coupled with my eternal optimism would prevail no matter how grim my circumstances may have looked.

At the time, I was a proponent of what is called in some circles, positive confession; a system whereby one uses Bible scriptures in concert with a positive confession to create their reality. I had successfully used the techniques of that system to land my first IT position, so I felt it was only a matter of time before I would prevail with this system again.

Before I started my job search each morning, I would look in the mirror and quote a scripture and talk to myself in Christian verbiage. I would blurt out phrases like, "I'm blessed and highly favored!" Then I would follow that up with my declaration that I would be hired by a technology company. It seems so silly now. Is God really moved by such things? Imagine my son or daughter standing in front of a mirror reciting positive thoughts in order to invoke a robotic favorable response from me!

Well, this time neither the positive-confession system, nor my optimism, worked for me. After all of my confessions and after striving to maintain a positive attitude, I was still under-employed or unemployed. At one point, I applied for public assistance and, due to my lack of insurance, was forced to take my son to the county hospital for medical care. Moreover, my sporadic work schedule and the demands of family life made it increasingly difficult to excel academically. Consequently, I had spent the last three quarters on academic probation and was now facing expulsion from UCI.

Now remember, this book isn't about God helping you find a job. Again, for me and for you, it's never really about finding a job; it's about finding God, while finding a job. God desires that we know him and see him as much as we can given the limits of our human understanding.

I thought that I knew God. I thought that I understood the rules that governed his interaction with his creation, but my understanding of God was based on false assumptions and misinformation. And when I could not manipulate God by formulas, when God failed to stay in the box that I placed him in, I felt abandoned. It's that feeling of abandonment that connects me to David's encounter with Ahimelech.

Now when Ahimelech asked the seemingly redundant question, "Why are you alone? Why is no one with you?" he was not attempting to make a profound statement. He simply wanted to know why a prominent man like David would not be traveling with an entourage. But sometimes the most cutting and profound statements are uttered in innocence. The question that Ahimelech posed to David is a question that we may need to ask ourselves from time to time.

When we feel isolated and cut off from God we tend to conjure up all sorts of ideas about God that are unproductive and false. We often think about what we did wrong to fall out of God's good graces, as if our doing right was the sole purpose for God's past blessings. We tear ourselves down and we beat ourselves up over the mistakes that we made or we begin to focus on the individual or circumstance that we think is responsible for our hardship.

David was beginning to travel down the road of doubt and despair. He began to focus on his adversary, Saul[7]. He was tired, afraid and isolated. But know this, although he wasn't aware of it, David was alone for a good reason. It was during this season of David's life that he wrote many of the Psalms.

Yes, sometimes we are alone and no one is with us because we chased everyone away. But that isn't always the case. There are times when we are alone so that we might learn in private what we will share in public. David conquered Goliath publicly and was ceremoniously thrust into the spotlight. Most books about faith begin and end with David's public victory over Goliath and omit David's private struggles as a fugitive.

[7] 1 Samuel 20:1

Do you feel isolated? Do you feel alone? Do you feel like no one is with you? I can relate to that feeling. But know this, more often than not, God will choose the privacy of the valley over the height of the mountain to develop our relationship with him. So after David defeated Goliath he didn't graduate from the school of faith, he enrolled in the next course, where his relationship with God deepened.

I don't know what course you are enrolled in at this moment. Perhaps you may feel like you are isolated or maybe you feel like God has kicked you to the curb. I do know that my season of isolation had a purpose. I would not be who I am today without the divine correction that I received when I thought I was alone.

In my season of despair, my theology underwent a divine makeover. I had been placing my faith in faith rather than placing my faith in God. That is to say, though I would affirm that God was the supreme sovereign Lord of the universe, my behavior suggested otherwise. Oh, if you could have seen me creating my reality in the mirror. I believed that God was subservient to my unbridled zeal through the power of my words;

utter nonsense. In my season of unwelcomed hardship, I found out that God's eternal purposes trumped my eternal optimism.

Before David killed his giant with zeal and optimism, he uttered this positive confession, "The LORD who rescued me from the paw of the lion and the paw of the bear will rescue me from the hand of this Philistine."[8] I believed that David's success and my success rested completely in a positive declaration and a positive attitude. God was using this trial to give me a better understanding of his word and himself.

I needed to know that God is relational, not mechanical. I was taught that you better watch every word you utter. If your words snare you, God can't help you, but nothing could be farther from the truth. The same David that hurled a positive confession at Goliath made many negative pronouncements as well.[9] David's negative confessions did not change God's plan for him. God wasn't suddenly rendered helpless because David, in

[8] 1 Samuel 17:37
[9] 1 Samuel 20:3

a moment of weakness, said what was on his heart. God isn't that small.

God is big; God is so big that he will bless us even when we don't deserve it. Sometimes our understanding is off, but God will still bless us. Sometimes we are disobedient, but God will bless us still.

After their emancipation from 400 years of bondage in Egypt, the Jewish people wandered in the wilderness for 40 years. On one occasion, during their wilderness wanderings, they were thirsty and there was no water in sight. To quench their thirst, God told Moses to speak to a rock in order to meet their need. Moses disobeyed God's command.[10] In anger, Moses didn't speak to the rock; Moses hit the rock. In spite of Moses's disobedience, God gave the thirsty nation water and dealt with Moses later.

I am not that big. When my kids make a mistake, most likely I will address it immediately. God doesn't work that way. First, God's compassion is greater than mine. Secondly, God is big enough to evaluate the present with an intimate knowledge of the future. But beyond that, God is more concerned with developing our hearts than controlling our behavior. When our hearts align with him, we will behave in a way that blesses him and blesses others.

After I landed my first IT position, I shared in God's glory by praising my positive confession. Fortunately, in every way, God is bigger than I. God knew that I would remain in the school of faith and that my next lesson would address my false assumptions regarding faith. Yes, God is much bigger than you and I. He wasn't pouting when I took part of his glory. He counted it as immaturity and worked it into his eternal plans for me.

Yes, I felt I was alone and no one was with me. But in reality, I was not alone. God was with me. He was just as present in my season of unemployment as he was in my second grade classroom. The same God who helped me defeat my giraffe; the same God that miraculously opened the door for me to enter the field of IT was still with me. You may feel alone, but someone is with you. And, as it was with David and me, there may be a divine eternal purpose behind your immediate need.

CHAPTER 4

Trials, Triggers & Divine Encounters

David asked Ahimelech, "Don't you have a spear or a sword here? I haven't brought my sword or any other weapon, because the king's mission was urgent. The priest replied, "The sword of Goliath the Philistine, whom you killed in the Valley of Elah, is here; it is wrapped in a cloth behind the ephod. If you want it, take it; there is no sword here but that one. "David said, "There is none like it; give it to me." [11]

Landing on the moon had become routine in 1970, but when an explosion occurred that crippled the spacecraft, suddenly the Apollo 13 mission to the moon became one of the most captivating space flights in history. The explosion triggered a series of suspenseful events that were depicted in the movie Apollo 13. There

[11] 1 Samuel 21:8-9

is a scene in that movie that captures the spirit of this chapter.

When the explosion occurred and it became clear that the lives of the crew were most likely lost, the movie shifts focus from the drama in the spacecraft to a pre-flight interview where one of the astronauts shares a war story. As he recounts his experience of a lost fighter pilot running out of fuel over the Pacific Ocean, you can sense his fear and vulnerability. Composed with a bit of uncertainty in his voice he utters these words "You never know what events will transpire to get you home." Those words are filled with truth that has stayed with me from the moment I heard them.

David was lost. When he encountered Ahimelech, he was spiritually and emotionally exhausted. His conflict with Saul had worn him down and erased the memory of his many victories. He forgot that God helped him overcome wild animals; he forgot that God helped him kill a giant; but most of all, he forgot that he was a favored son. As a result, he began to expect less and less from God, eventually he didn't expect anything at all. David was no longer living a supernatural life; he was reduced to simply trying to survive from day to day. The optimism, faith, and zeal that marked David in his classic confrontation with Goliath were replaced with fear, hopelessness, isolation and compromise. In the passage above, we see David resorting to lies. He wasn't running errands for the King; he was running from the King.

Can you relate to David here? Are you familiar with his by-any-means-necessary obsession with self-preservation? Have you ever lived in the illusion that God has deserted you? Do you know what it is like to forget about the bear, the lion and giant that God helped you defeat?

Maybe you excelled in college or trade school but you are not having the same success in the job market. Perhaps you were laid off from an executive or management position and you can't seem to find a comparable position with another company.

When you are working an unskilled job for very low wages or not working at all, you tend to forget about that excellent term paper that you wrote in college. After many unsuccessful attempts to gain employment, you can forget that you were once a valued contributor to the success of a company. After a while, lack of success and repeated failure can erase your greatest triumphs.

I know how David felt when he encountered Ahimelech. I understand why he lied to obtain food and a spear. That's where I was before God intervened in my Valley of Elah. In my case, the Valley of Elah was a department store in Orange County, California, and my Ahimelech was a well-dressed suburban woman. In that department store, like the lost fighter pilot turned astronaut, I learned that you never know what events will transpire to get you home. It's that God-scripted story that I want to share with you in this chapter.

I was in desperate need of a trigger that would restore my trust in God. As I stated in the previous chapter, when my internship ended, I had a hard time landing another IT position. Consequently, while I continued pursing my computer science degree, I had to take any and every type of work I could find to support my family.

I worked nights as a security guard, and I also worked through a temporary agency. I worked as a dishwasher, a telemarketer, a drill-press operator, a stock clerk, and a host of other odd jobs. I'm not putting down anyone who works in any of the fields that I mentioned. Simply stated, I wasn't a very good dishwasher, drill-press operator, stock clerk, or telemarketer. I broke a lot of dishes, I stocked a lot of packages on the wrong shelves, and I drilled a lot of holes in the wrong places. Sometimes we don't succeed at one thing because we are destined for something else.

Besides the instability that often accompanies unskilled temporary work, there was something else that I found even more troubling. This season of my life was a huge blow to my ego. Like David I was experiencing a great fall from grace.

Before David was reduced to a hunted fugitive in the Valley of Elah, he was the pride of Israel. Women would literally burst into song when he entered the city gates.[12] With the ladies, David was the teen heartthrob of his era. At the same time, because he defeated Goliath, he garnered the respect of the men, as well.

[12] 1Ssamuel 18:6-7

Because I had been an engineer for a highly respected company, intern or otherwise, people held me in high regard. When I showed up for work in my Sunday best, I felt like I was somebody. The African Americans that worked for the company, the older ones in particular, would acknowledge me with a nod, as if to say, "You are making us proud, Son." However, when my employment ended, so did my prestige and self-worth. Suddenly I wasn't an up-and-coming young professional on a fast track; I was a struggling young father trying to keep my head above water. Although this trying time was unwelcomed, I can see now that it was one of the most constructive seasons of my life. How I see people, how I see myself and, most importantly, how I see God, was greatly shaped during this difficult time.

I was facing huge headwinds financially and in my marriage that made it difficult to improve my academic standing. I was expelled from college. When I received my dismissal letter from the university, I felt it was time to give up on any career in IT. I had reached my tipping point, and in my mind, my pursuit of an IT career had ended. So I decided to ask my father, a custodian for the Los Angeles Unified School District , to pull some strings to get me an entry-level janitorial position. However, before I could carry out my plan, God set his plan in motion.

At some point, during this trying season of my life, I stopped looking for an IT position and I was working as a department store cashier. Like the rest of the jobs that I worked for over a year now, the pay wasn't great. In fact, when the payroll department failed to print my first payroll check, my manager paid me from the petty cash drawer. In less than a year, I went from an automatic payroll deposit to receiving my wages from the petty cash drawer. I knew that I wasn't making a living wage, but the petty cash drawer poured salt in my wounds.

In my IT position, I had grown accustomed to being seen. But now, I was working a job where people rarely made eye contact with me. My cashier's job was possibly the most invisible job of all my invisible jobs.

As a cashier, the department store required me to enthusiastically greet the customers with phrases like, "How are you today?" and to send them off with something like, "Have a wonderful day!" Now when you put yourself out there like that and someone just blows their nose and walks away, that can mess with you.

One day, while I was going through the motions of blurting out my enthusiastic mechanical greetings and parting phrases to customers. God decided that it was time to jump start my faith and take our relationship to another level. As I was settling in to my invisibleness, brought on by a series of non-responsive customers, a special female customer came through the line.

She began her dialogue with a warm smile and these words, "Are you Darryl Brumfield? Darryl, how have you been?" Those words were music to my ears; I had heard them before and instantly I was reminded of our first encounter. The woman in the line worked for the company that hired me under the pretense that I was another Darryl Brumfield. She was the same woman who greeted me at the reception desk when I showed up to interview for the IT internship.

I quickly realized that this scene was not a coincidence it was a divine appointment. The woman in line was my priest pointing me to my sword (my faith) that I used to kill bears and slay the giants and the checkout line was my Elah. Once again, God set me up. This woman was God's instrument. When I was ready to give up, God sent her to remind me that I had conquered giants and that I was still a favored son. We spoke briefly, but because I believed that our meeting was a divine encounter, when she encouraged me to continue my education and pursuit of a career in IT, her words hit their mark with pinpoint accuracy.

Again, it wasn't as if she said something that was astounding. In fact, others had said the same thing. But, before faith matured into activity, doubt would always overtake their words. So God orchestrated the events so that my faith would get the jump on my doubt. The woman standing in front of me was God's instrument transporting me to a time and place where I had experienced God's hilarious unconventional favor.

Within weeks of that encounter, I was enrolled into a Junior college to continue my IT education and I also started looking for entry-level IT positions. And after a few more failed attempts to gain employment in the IT field, I landed an entry-level computer programing position.

When David had lost hope because of his long trial, God arranged a divine appointment with the priest at Elah for him. The priest had something that no one else had; the sword that David used to slay Goliath. But it wasn't enough to inform David that the sword of Goliath was there. No, the priest added, "...it is wrapped in a cloth behind the ephod. If you want it, take it".[13]

The question prompted David to take action. Like David, after I was reminded of God's favor, I took action. I decided to continue my IT career. When God gives you faith, you need to use it in the moment, and that is what I did. No formulas, no standing in front of a mirror reciting canned phrases like a parrot. I just rested in the fact God saw me, in the security of that place; I knew that he would open the right door at the right time.

At the end of the day, my transition from my first IT internship to my season of invisible jobs to my first full-time, non-intern IT position, like every job transition in my professional career, wasn't about employment.

[13] 1 Samuel 21:9

Again, it doesn't take God days, months, or years to find you or me a job. But sometimes it does take days, months, and years to find God as he is revealed in scripture. And it takes time to find our identity in God. And maybe God is doing just that in your long trial. I needed to learn by experience that God wasn't my Genie, and I needed to divorce my identity from my title and my position in this world. My identity and self-worth is rooted in my position in God's family and God's kingdom.

In conclusion, have you stopped asking God for help? Have you stopped expecting anything from him? If so, I know that God doesn't want you to stay in that place. I also know that He will visit you in that place. So when He shows up in a way that sparks your faith, don't pass it off as a coincidence. No, take it as a sign that God isn't through working out his grand plan in you. God hasn't abandoned you. If you were his favored child, you are his favored child, still.

CHAPTER 5

Job Security, Insecurity & God's Ability

A champion named Goliath, who was from Gath, came out of the Philistine camp. His height was six cubits and a span. He had a bronze helmet on his head and wore a coat of scale armor of bronze weighing five thousand shekels; on his legs he wore bronze greaves, and a bronze javelin was slung on his back. His spear shaft was like a weaver's rod, and its iron point weighed six hundred shekels. His shield bearer went ahead of him. Goliath stood and shouted to the ranks of Israel, "Why do you come out and line up for battle?... On hearing the Philistine's words, Saul and all the Israelites were dismayed and terrified... As he was talking with them, Goliath, the Philistine champion from Gath, stepped out from his lines and shouted his usual defiance, and David heard it. Whenever the Israelites saw the man, they all fled from him in great fear... David asked the men standing near him, "What will be done for the man who kills this Philistine and removes this disgrace from Israel? Who is this uncircumcised Philistine that he should defy the armies of the living God?"[14]

[14] 1 Samuel 17:4-8,11,23,24,26

Jim Brown, the Hall of Fame Cleveland Browns running back, would intimidate and defeat his opponents before the game even started. During the pre-game warm up, Jim Brown loved to show off his superior strength and agility. Because of his pre-game antics, Jim Brown broke some tackles before the opening kickoff.

Like Jim Brown, Goliath used intimidation to paralyze Israel's army. While the men of Israel hid in their fox holes, Goliath showed off his physical attributes and taunted them.[15] His stature and the size of his weapons were impressive, and the sight of them filled the hearts of Israelites with fear, but David was not afraid; Goliath's egotism did not intimidate David. Yes, Goliath was strong, but in David's eyes circumcision trumped physical strength.

Circumcision wasn't a common practice. To Goliath and the rest of the ancient world circumcision may have appeared to be a senseless superstitious bloody act, but it was much more than that to David. For David,

---

[15] 1 Samuel 17:9-10

circumcision was a physical sign to remind him that the Israelites had a unique relationship with God.

David believed that he and his countrymen were beneficiaries of the favor that God showed to their ancestor Abraham. As God was with Abraham, God would be with them. If God helped Abraham defeat his enemies, God would help his descendants defeat their enemies. In David's mind, it simply boiled down to this truth. Goliath was uncircumcised and, therefore, he was outside of this special relationship. Goliath may have thought that his physical superiority and impressive armaments gave him an advantage, but he was deceived.

The entire army of Israel made the delusion of Goliath their reality, but David did not buy what Goliath was selling. David rested in the special relationship that he had with God. David knew that God had his back. If you are a child of God, you have a special relationship with God and God has your back.

It's a great feeling to know that God has your back. Fear will always box you in. Fear compels you to hide in your bunker, but when you know that God has your back, there is liberty. When you know that God has your back, you are free to make moves and take risks.

Unfortunately, like the Israeli soldiers who were intimidated by Goliath, most people live out their life stuck in foxholes. Pastors are often paralyzed by parishioners and business people are often paralyzed by old paradigms. After my season of odd jobs ended, I was paralyzed. When I landed my first non-intern IT position, my job became my foxhole.

Over the years, I have listened to many people tell me how much they dread their job. Yet, because of fear of the unknown, these same people would never pursue greener pastures. They chose to remain in a rut and complain about their lot rather than do something about it. For many people, their choice is a byproduct of something called job security.

Have you ever felt like you were stuck in a job due to job security? After working for six years in my second IT position, I was bunkered down in my job security foxhole. I needed a paradigm shift; I needed to change my view of employment. The next job story is about how God supplied the paradigm shift that released me from my self-made prison.

While working in my second IT position, I developed an unhealthy dependence on my employer. Two factors fed my unhealthy dependence: tradition and fear. I was afraid of the host of risks associated with a job change, and I was hesitant to act outside the norm of my cultural roots.

There were a number of issues related to changing jobs that I didn't want to deal with. I might not find favor with my new employer or the new company might go under. If that happened, I might repeat my season of odd jobs. Still, in the end, it was my cultural traditions that handcuffed me to my second IT position.

I was raised in a culture that encouraged you to never quit a good job. When you got a good job, you worked that job until you died. My dad and uncles worked for the same employers for their entire adult lives. My sister, who was a source of encouragement for me, was once considered a reckless rebel because she quit a government job. She left a position with the county of Los Angeles to pursue an exciting career in the travel industry. Now that was something you never did. You never quit a good government job!

Job security is not a bad thing. However, because I was using job security to mask my insecurities, job security was a bad thing for me. I saw the company I worked for as my provider. In reality, the company was just the instrument by which God provided for physical needs.

After working in my second IT position for six years, my comfort zone had become a prison. I was a company man; I was completely dependent on the company to fulfill my needs. I trusted the company more than I trusted God. So, to correct my warped thinking, God enrolled me in another course in the school of faith.

In the sixth year of my employment with the company, Rick was hired. Rick was a really sharp college graduate from a very prestigious school. Although Rick and I came from completely different backgrounds, within a short time we became good friends. As our friendship developed, I felt comfortable discussing my desire to pursue a better opportunity with him.

While working for the company, I honed my programming skills, but I had outgrown my current position. A company called Microsoft had just come out with a new product called Windows, and I had a hunch that I needed to become proficient in programming this new technology. I also felt that I needed a raise in salary. Over the past six years, I had received raises at about 6 percent per year. When you factored in my modest starting salary, my salary was far below market value for someone with my technical skills.

One day I shared my discontent with my current position and my aspirations for greener pastures with Rick. Without hesitation, he challenged me to do something about it. I responded to his challenge by rambling off a bunch of excuses that made me look small and made my God seem even smaller, but Rick was really persistent and persuasive.

Looking back, I really feel that God sent Rick into my life to rattle my cage. Because of Rick's input, I decided to take a leap of faith and explore new opportunities. This was the first of many free falls in my employment history.

Free-falling is a great experience. When I was growing, up the older women would describe free-falling with the phrase, "Let go and let God." Well, I let go of my second IT position. I didn't physically quit the job, but I let go of the job mentally. The job was no longer my provider. Having released the job in my heart, I was ready to receive with open arms whatever God wanted to do with my career.

In reality, we can never "let God." God is always at work. But when we, "let go," we become willing participants in the great work God is doing, and we get a courtside seat to God's handiwork.

After I decided to test the job market, I landed a part-time consulting position in about a week's time. After a few months of moonlighting, I was offered a full-time position. I accepted the offer and began my stint of employment with my third IT company.

My new position was superior to my previous position. I received a 15 percent increase in salary, and I was learning a new technology. Instead of programming a proprietary user-interface (UI), I was learning how to program the UI that I had been reading about called

Windows. But two months after accepting the full-time position, the company was sold and that's when the free-falling really began.

As you might have guessed, staff changes followed, and I became a casualty of the acquisition. However, the way in which I was notified that my services were no longer needed turned out to be one of my many on-the-job God moments.

Although I had only known my manager for a few months, he really felt bad about letting me go. In fact, my termination happened in the following manner. I was asked out to lunch and in the midst of stuffing my face, my manager broke down and cried. I asked, "What's wrong? Are you okay?" But he just kept sobbing. Finally, he wiped his nose and said, "Darryl, in eight weeks I will have to let you go." Then he started up with the tears once more. It was Niagara Falls all over. As I was consoling him, I remembered thinking to myself, "Man, there is something wrong with this picture. I'm the one that's getting terminated; shouldn't someone pass me a tissue?"

My manager was a Christian. He had come to enjoy our talks about faith and life, and he didn't want this to end abruptly or with any type of bitterness or malice. For about a half hour, I told him time and time again that God was in control. That God only wanted our paths to cross for this brief time. That time had now come to an abrupt end.

So now the clock was ticking. I had eight weeks to find another job. I quickly put together a resume. Confident that I could find a job within eight weeks, I started my job search the next day. Before I knew it, seven weeks flew by and I still had not found a job.

As I was cleaning out my desk on the last day of my last week of employment, I received a phone call from my previous employer. It turned out that they wanted to build a Windows version of their application and they wanted me to lead the development effort.

Their competitor had announced that they would release a Windows version of their product at the industry's largest trade show, which was coming up in four months. To keep pace with the competition, they needed a Windows version of their product and they were willing to pay a premium to get it.

The job offer went something like this, "Darryl, I'm going to be honest with you. We don't have time to bring someone else up to speed. You wrote the old code for the old product and we need you to convert it to Windows. What will it take to get you to come back? We are willing to pay you more than you are receiving from your current employer. So Darryl, what is it going to take?"

Well, if they had called after I cleaned out my desk it would have taken a lot less. Technically, I was still on the payroll for another couple of hours, so I gave him my current salary. Then I was told that they could beat that salary by 15, maybe 20 percent. My former manager then said "would 15 percent do it?" I paused to take it all in, and then before I could respond he blurted out, "Okay 20 percent. That's as high as I think I can go." After that exchange, he quickly got off the phone to start setting the wheels in motion for my offer letter, but there was a hitch.

I had only been away from my second IT position for just two months, and in the interim they had hired a new general manager, named Jimmy. He was a tough-nosed ex-military man that had been hired to streamline every aspect of the company. Now Jimmy could not understand how I could be worth 46 percent more than I was worth just over two months earlier.

You see, I left the company two weeks after I had received my annual 6 percent raise. The offer that I accepted was 15 percent above my annual 6 percent raise, and now I was being offered 20 percent above that to return. Cutting to the chase, before I could be hired back, I had to meet with Jimmy. In that meeting I needed to prove to him that I had increased my market value by 46 percent in just 10 weeks!

I showed up the next day and met with my former manager prior to my meeting with Jimmy. My former manager was really nervous and I could tell that there was some tension between him and Jimmy. He shared some of his concerns with me. The conversation went something like this, "Darryl, Jimmy just doesn't get it. He just doesn't understand software. He doesn't understand that I can't afford to spend three to four weeks interviewing other candidates. Then there is the training and the team chemistry. Darryl, Jimmy just doesn't get it." After he filled my backpack with his concerns, a secretary interrupted our conversation and escorted me into Jimmy's office.

As I walked down the hallway, I could tell that everyone revered Jimmy. In fact, as I was walking down the hall someone nodded their head and said in a somber voice, "Good luck with Jimmy." When I entered Jimmy's office, immediately I knew what all the fuss was about. Right away I noticed that Jimmy was a stern, no-nonsense, former military officer who ran a tight ship.

In a very stern voice Jimmy said, "Darryl, I'm going to get right to the point, I don't know how you're worth 46 percent more than what we paid you just 10 weeks ago. And what will stop you from leaving us in ten weeks for the next best offer?"

Caught somewhat off guard by Jimmy's bluntness, I just responded with the honest truth. In a soft spoken tone, I said, "Well, a lot of prayer and thought went into my decision to leave the company ten weeks ago." Then, before I could make another statement, Jimmy looking surprised and enthused, uttered these words, "Prayer, did you say prayer?," before reclining back into his oversized chair.

It turns out that that Jimmy was an old-school, tongue-talking Pentecostal Christian who really believed in the power of faith and prayer. Consequently, I never had to explain to Jimmy why my market value increased 46 percent in ten weeks. He figured it out all by himself, and graciously shared his answer with me. "Darryl," he said. "I know why you are worth 46 percent more than you were 10 weeks ago. You are a King's kid!"

Jimmy retired about a year later, and on his last day with the company he pulled me aside to remind me of our first encounter. Placing his hand on my shoulder he said, "Darryl, never let fear control you and never forget that you are a King's kid." I am eternally grateful for his counsel.

The takeaway from this story is not how to get a 46 percent increase in salary in 10 weeks. No, this chapter is about liberty, the kind of liberty that comes with knowing that you are a King's kid and this is where my story intersects with David's. David had this liberty. That is what compelled him to run toward his giant and defeat him.

God doesn't want us to be stuck in foxholes because we are afraid of unknown giants. He wants us to trust him and take some risks. Trusting God may usher in a season of uncertainty. You may experience a free fall and you may feel some anxiety when you don't see the landmarks that you're accustomed to. But you will find liberty, and you will experience God's power and God's provision.

Know this, like the running back Jim Brown, Goliaths will parade their strength in front of you. Your relationship with God will not stop giants from trying to intimidate you. We really don't have much control over that. However, we can decide whether or not we will adhere to the voices that quench our faith. The choice is ours. We can complain about our lot and hide in the false security of our foxhole, or we take some risks knowing that God has our backs.

CHAPTER 6

Armed & Precarious

Then Saul dressed David in his own tunic. He put a coat of armor on him and a bronze helmet on his head. David fastened on his sword over the tunic and tried walking around, because he was not used to them. "I cannot go in these," he said to Saul, "because I am not used to them." So he took them off. [16]

Saul had the very best intentions; wanting to increase David's odds of achieving a victory over Goliath, Saul gave David the best armor available. David, without any resistance, accepted Saul's armor and suited up. But after taking the armor for a test drive, David realized he was better off without it.

[16] 1 Samuel 17:38-39

David's refusal to wear Saul's armor was not an indictment against armor; David wore armor in subsequent battles. It's a prudent thing to protect oneself when going into a battle. However, at this point in David's life, God was laying a foundation, a foundation of faith that he would continually build upon. For now, wearing armor would circumvent David's spiritual development. By faith David killed a lion, by faith he killed a bear. Faith's reward would not be a coat of armor. Instead, David's reward for exercising faith would be more faith. Does that reward excite you?

About two years after I returned to the IT company that ended my season of unskilled labor; the company was sold to a holding company. The acquisition disrupted the working environment for the worse. In a cold and decisive manner, the new owners terminated about 20 percent of the employees. Jimmy, my mentor and friend, was one of the first to go. But Jimmy was one of the lucky ones; he had a golden parachute and advance notice. Others were not as fortunate.

After being huddled into an area in the manufacturing area, one by one each employee was called into an office. After they entered the office, they received an envelope that contained either a pink slip or an offer letter. I still remember the tears and the toil that accompanied that day as I watched my coworkers open their envelopes and discover their fate. It was like I was living a Roger Moore documentary.

In the following months, the morale at that company went from bad to worse. Consequently, although the new management desired to retain my services, I decided to pursue an employment opportunity elsewhere.

In one sense, I was making progress. For the first time in my life, to pursue a better opportunity, I was willing to quit a good-paying job. Like my older sister, who left a good government job, I too was a rebel and it felt great.

Although I was not aware of it at the time, the abrupt and severe layoffs that I had witnessed impacted my faith in a negative way. Consequently, God used another on-the-job teaching moment to put me back on the right track. My next lesson in the school of faith began when I accepted an IT position from a small IT company in the area.

On face value, for a number of reasons, changing employers didn't make a lot of sense. To begin with, the opportunity for advancement in my new position was less than or, at best, equal to my current position. The new position wouldn't expose me to a new technology, there was only a nominal difference in salary and benefits and the future of my new employer was extremely precarious. Nevertheless, because the layoff went down the way that it did, I was compelled to overlook the negatives and change jobs.

My new employer was one of the small assets of the late Robert Maxwell's large estate, which included several companies in the UK and in the US. Unfortunately, greed may have gotten the best of Robert Maxwell. Allegedly, before he went missing at sea, he embezzled money from his employee's pension fund. To compensate those harmed by Robert Maxwell's actions, his estate was seized and ordered to be liquidated to satisfy his debts. With his larger assets already sold, the trustees were looking to unload his smaller assets within the next six months.

Although the future of my new employer was uncertain, there was one aspect of their offer letter that made the company attractive to me. The company was offering a one-year severance package for employees who were terminated as a consequence of the pending sale of the company. This benefit was put in place so that the company could sustain operations, during the search for a buyer.

Now having experienced a corporate takeover, I felt that this little stipulation gave me a 50-50 chance of obtaining income insurance for at least one year. My confidence in job security had been shattered. So, I thought, what do I have to lose? If I get laid off, I would be laid off in style—the golden parachute. Well maybe not golden, but at least I would have a parachute.

In harmony with my plans, the Company was sold to a software company in London, England. Our employee agreement stipulated that we could not be relocated beyond 75 miles from our facility in Costa

Mesa, Calif. Consequently, when the acquisition was announced, it felt like Christmas Eve when I was 12.

My heart was filled with joyous expectation. If I were to be abruptly laid off, I would still have an income stream for a whole year. Certainly, I could find a job within one year. I felt like I had enough armor to protect me. I could take a breather and relax now. I would not be stressed by the threat of unemployment anymore. I welcomed unemployment because it would provide enough armor to shield me from financial ruin.

I begin to think about what I would do to fill my time, in the event that I was laid off by the new owners of the company. As I searched for a new employment opportunity, I would read some books or maybe even write one. I could just see myself walking along the beach and meditating on my favorite scriptures or taking that family vacation that I always wanted to take.

My excitement over the pending purchase of the company by a London-based corporation was shared by my coworkers. A few of the administrative staff were shown the door on the day of the announcement. Unlike the previous layoff that I had experienced, this was a joyous day. Everyone had pep in their step as they exited the building. I was told that the technical staff would meet with management on the following day. I can't accurately describe how much I looked forward to my exit interview.

The next day I strolled into the office without a care in the world. Before I could take a seat at my desk, my manager, with a somewhat perplexed look on his face ask me to step into his office. Why is he so despondent? I wondered as I took my seat in his office. My curiosity was soon put to rest when my manager began to talk.

"Darryl, I'll get right to point. The new owners have decided to retain the services of the technical management team and the key engineers." Now there are times when a very simple phrase can sound really complicated. This was one of those times. Immediately, after hearing his opening statement, I began to process the word "key" to determine rather or not my role in the company fit the criteria of "key engineer." My deduction ended when my manager uttered his next phrase. "Darryl, you have been identified as a key engineer."

For about a week I was pretty disappointed that I was a "key engineer." My plan had failed. Instead of a much-needed rest from the rat race, I was an employee of a company whose future was uncertain. Once again, I would need God's help to guide me through the wilderness of employment.

There is an event that took place during the wilderness wanderings of the nation of Israel that is closely related to what I was going through. After being delivered from bondage in Egypt, they were guided through the wilderness supernaturally by a fire by night and a cloud by day. That sure beats any GPS system that we have today. Yet, Moses decided to trade in their supernatural guide for a human one. His name was Hobab.[17] Moses' decision underscores the human condition. No matter how gracious God has been, we sometimes suffer from spiritual amnesia.

God had shown me so much favor in meeting all of my needs. In a very special way, he had launched my career in computer science. When my back was against

[17] Numbers 10:29-31

the wall, time and time again, he had demonstrated both his sovereignty and his faithfulness toward me. Since the day that I hurriedly entered into marriage, I had been living by faith. God had proven himself a faithful guide and provider. Yet, like Moses, I wanted to depend on a resource that I could see. The one-year severance package was my Hobab.

Unlike David, I wanted my armor. Yes, I was looking forward to spending some quality time with my family and enjoying some great downtime with God, as well. But what I wanted most of all from the severance package was a sabbatical from faith because I had become weary of trusting God to supply my needs.

There is nothing wrong with having a savings account, life insurance, education, investments or a prudent financial plan for your family's future. It's wise to have an earthquake kit in your home and a spare tire in the trunk of your car. God can use all of these instruments. In fact, whenever I had a flat tire, God used my spare tire, my run flat tires or my Auto Club card to deliver me. Again, the issue isn't the armor; it's trusting in the armor.

The problem with Moses, me and maybe you boils down to a shift in faith from God to something else. My problem was thinking that my war chest would be large enough to replace God. My reasoning rested on a fallacy. Simply stated, we don't know what the future holds for us; therefore, we really don't know whether or not we can declare our independence from God.

Yes, our Hobabs may be able to guide us through the foreseen obstacles that we might find along the way. But there are enemies and obstacles that we cannot see. What we can't foresee may be strong enough to penetrate our armor and is often greater than our Hobabs. A latter event in David's life drives this point home.

King David was a man of faith, but at the end of his life he had a setback in faith. He took a census, something that God did not want him to do.[18] His disobedience led to the death of 70,000 men. At first glance one might say: "What is wrong with taking a census? What is wrong with doing a head count?"

[18] 2 Samuel 24:1-24

Well, if determining the appropriate amount of government services is the motive for the head count, there is nothing wrong with taking a census. But David's motive for taking a census was not related to social services, it was about the size of his war chest. The size of David's kingdom was his Hobab and his armor.

God had given David victories when he had a small army of about 400 men. And God's favor continued to be with him as his armies and his stature grew.[19] But now David was looking to the size of his army to give him a false sense of security. In his mind, for once in his life, instead of playing the role of the underdog, he could go into battles as the favorite. The size of his army would prevent his enemies from attacking him. God graciously gave David a reality check by reducing the size of his army.

Remember, this is the same David who defeated a giant, a giant that defied an entire army. This is the same David that declined to wear Saul's armor. But David, like you and I, lived in a material world. Consequently, he was

<hr>

[19] 1 Samuel 22:2

tempted to rely on something tangible, something that he could see, and sometimes David failed the test.

Nevertheless, God loves us so much that he will not allow you or me to drop out of the school of faith. David forgot the lesson from his youth. He forgot that the reward for using faith is more faith. Faith, like a muscle, must be exercised otherwise it will suffer from atrophy. God wasn't going to allow my severance package to get in the way of working my faith muscles.

Now I am not suggesting that God is opposed to prosperity. In the end, prosperity or scarcity is not the key issue. There are people who are destitute in the world's eyes, but they have great faith in God. There are also people who have great wealth in the world's eyes, yet they also have great faith in God. In my case, I needed correction.

After a few years of living from hand to mouth, I wanted a break—the same break that so many people seek today. I no longer wanted to depend on God to make a way for me. With the severance package, I would have enough armor to make away for myself. Maybe that's where you are today. You feel you need a faith sabbatical. Like Moses, David and me, you just want a little break from faith.

I was deceived. Sometimes we can think that we are sufficiently armed when in fact we are not. I was more vulnerable with the severance package and no faith than I was without the severance package with faith. The truth is, there isn't a nest egg, insurance policy or career track that is equal to God. The severance package was a finite resource that could be exhausted with one unexpected event. God, on the other hand, is an inexhaustible resource.

Moving forward I would not look for a faith sabbatical. Like David, I disposed of my material armor and embraced the uncertainty ahead, knowing that I was sufficiently armed with God's promises. My faith in God would provide all the protection that I would ever need.

CHAPTER 7

The Master's Degree vs. The Master's Decree

"So David triumphed over the Philistine with a sling and a stone; without a sword in his hand he struck down the Philistine and killed him."[20]

Shortly after what I thought was my exit interview, my new employers revealed their plans for both the company and its key engineers. They decided to move all software development to the UK. After one year, coinciding with the expiration of a lucrative severance package, the California software development office would be closed. Consequently, all of the engineers based in California, including myself, were looking for

---

[20] 1 Samuel 17:50

employment opportunities elsewhere. Mike was one of the engineers on my team who was looking to jump ship.

Mike was using the Veteran's tuition program to pay for his master's degree, which he planned to complete in a month or so. I knew this because Mike spoke of it constantly. There wasn't a day that went by that Mike did not share his grand plan with his coworkers. He was so looking forward to the date when he could state on his resume that he had a master's degree. He would often say, "When they see my degree complete date, they will see that I am a go-getter. They will see that I wanted to separate myself from the crowd."

I really envied Mike; I thought it would be really nice to be in Mike's position. In a month or so he would have a master's degree and that degree would make him extremely marketable. In contrast, I didn't have a degree. The last institution that I graduated from was Dominguez High School in Compton, California. I began to see Mike and all of the other engineers, who possessed at least a bachelor's degree, as having more options than myself. If Mike's resume said that he was a "go-getter," what did my resume say?

I began to focus on the formal educational gap between Mike, the other engineers in the office and myself. My preoccupation with my lack of credentials wasn't healthy and eventually it impacted my job search. Thinking that I was unqualified as I searched for employment, I disregarded the job descriptions and focused on the college degree requirement. I didn't look for opportunities that matched my interest and skill set. Instead, I looked for any employer willing to give me a job. It was at this point that God orchestrated a series of events that forever change my warped thinking.

Early one morning, while I was sipping on a cup of coffee and reviewing my scheduled tasks, I was abruptly interrupted by Mike. "Darryl, my degree is already paying dividends! And I haven't even graduated yet," he blurted out.

Mike was excited. He was on the verge of being hired by one of the up-and-coming software companies in the area. His resume, due in part to his pending master's degree, had allowed him to clear the first hurdle. And after two successful technical interviews, the only thing that stood between Mike and a great opportunity was a reference check.

After he took his seat in the cubicle next to me, he spent the next 20 minutes telling me about his great opportunity. He talked about the stock options, the work environment, the salary and the technology. On every level this company was far superior to our current company.

When Mike concluded his monologue, he told me that before drafting an offer letter, the company wanted to talk with someone that he had worked with recently. Since we had collaborated on a few projects, he suggested that the company contact me. Immediately after I found out that I was Mike's reference, my phone rang. The party on the other end of the phone line just happened to be a representative of the company that was interested in hiring Mike.

With Mike sitting two feet away, I proceeded to give him a glowing review. Mike was beaming as I boasted of his technical and analytical acumen. When the phone call ended, Mike thanked me for taking the time to give him such a favorable and gracious endorsement. At that point, I asked Mike if the company was looking to fill other positions. His response created a rather awkward moment.

Responding to my inquiry about a position, Mike stated, with a bit of regret in his voice, "Darryl, they would never hire you." Sensing that his remarks may have offended me, he quickly went on to say, "Darryl, I hope you didn't take that wrong way. What I meant to say is that this company will only consider candidates that have a technical degree. In fact, they prefer candidates that hold master's degrees. I'll have a master's degree in a few months. Since you don't have a technical degree, they wouldn't consider you for a position; that's all I meant."

"Oh, it's okay Mike; no offence taken." I stated rather calmly with a bit of a smile. But to be honest, I was trying my best to hide my emotions. Although I appeared to be reserved, I was excited and overwhelmed with delightful expectation. My delight was rooted in the simple prayer that was in my heart and on my lips. You see, Mike caused me to reflect on a past time, a previous experience where God, in spite of my weakness, showed his strength. The greatest spoil from this past victory was a simple prayer. So when the opportunity presented itself, I turned away from Mike and whispered these sweet words in God's ear, "Lord, show yourself strong."

The prayer is not a command. God doesn't take orders; he gives them. The prayer is an acknowledgement that my resources are insufficient for the task at hand. Our weakness simply provides God an opportunity to showcase his strength. Believe it or not, God is actually searching the earth for that kind of scenario.[21]

About two minutes after I prayed, Mike's phone started ringing. He picked up the phone and responded to the caller on the other end with the following words, "Yes, um, um, oh, okay. Thank you very much." When Mike hung up the phone, he turned to me and said, "Oh well. I guess I'll have to continue my search. They decided not to make me an offer." I replied, "Man, that's too bad. It seemed like a great opportunity." Then my phone started ringing.

[21] 2 Chronicles 16:9

My responses to the caller sounded curiously similar to Mike's responses. "Um, um, oh, okay, thank you very much." However, I was having a very different conversation with the caller. When I picked up the phone the woman on the other end said, "Hello, are you Darryl Brumfield? Well, I know our hiring manager called you regarding Mike's reference, but he really likes you and he thinks that you are the man for the job. He wants to meet with you as soon as possible."

When the phone call ended, Mike wanted to know who called me. I said, "It was the company that just called about your reference. They want me to come in for an interview." He responded, "Well, good luck; I wish you the best, but remember they turned me down and I practically have a master's degree." Apparently the Master's decree trumps a master's degree. At the end of the day, a simple petition that is in alignment with God's plan for you will overcome the deck that is stacked against you. After a successful interview, I was hired.

Now the moral of this story is not that education has no value. Daniel, who is most known for his trial in the Lion's den, excelled in the classroom.[22] It is clear that God used Daniel's education to strategically place him in the most prominent government position in the ancient Babylonian Empire; second only to the King himself.[23] All of my adult children have a college education, and at a later point in my career I completed my bachelor's degree. I understand the merits of pursuing a formal education; diminishing its value is not the takeaway from this chapter of my life.

I hope you take away this liberating truth; God, the Supreme Being in the whole universe, is looking for opportunities to frustrate the conventional wisdom of men. So don't pass on a great opportunity because you or someone else talked you out it by filling your head with doubt and your heart with fear. When your weaknesses or lack of qualifications are brought to your attention, don't throw in the towel. If God is for you, what you have, great or small, is all that you need. Like David, with a sling and a stone, you can defeat giants.

[22] Daniel 1:3-6,17-20
[23] Daniel 2:48

CHAPTER 8

From Mountain Top to Plateau

He then turned away to someone else and brought up the same matter, and the men answered him as before. What David said was overheard and reported to Saul, and Saul sent for him.[24]

I heard story about a reluctant cruise ship hero that went something like this. A man was enjoying the view on deck when he heard someone shout, "Man overboard!" Before he knew it, he was surrounded by fellow passengers. And soon, because of the frenzy to see the man in the water, he found himself pressed against the railing of the ship.

[24] 1Samuel 17:30

As the ship came to a halt, the man appeared to jump into the water to save the passenger that fell overboard. After this, a lifesaver was thrown into the water and both men were rescued. The second man in the water was praised for his heroism. After all, it took real courage to jump into the water and save the life of a total stranger.

When the captain of the ship heard that one passenger risked his life to save another, he decided to have dinner to honor the heroic passenger. So that evening the hero sat at the captain's table and enjoyed a dinner in his honor.

At the end of the evening, after talking about the virtue of valor, the captain asked the hero to join him at the podium to address his fellow passengers. The hero received a standing ovation. As he stood and sheepishly made his way to the podium, "Oh, what a humble man," said one passenger under their breath. "He must be awkward around crowds," said another.

When he reached the podium, he motioned with his hands for the cheering to stop, cleared his throat and said "I appreciate all of the accolades, but before I say anything, I need to ask a question." After a long pause, he said, "Who pushed me?" Let's face it, sometimes in this life we need a push to move beyond our comfort zone and experience great things. That push can come from friends or foes.

After many trials and tests, I was employed by one of the best IT companies in Orange County, California. If that wasn't enough, my morning commute to work was about 8 stress-free miles, a coveted commute for most people living in Southern California. My company provided an above-market salary and stock options. In addition to my monetary compensation, there were some extra perks.

My employer provided free soft drinks and snacks, including fresh-popped popcorn each Friday at 3 p.m. Pizza, egg rolls, and other finger foods and desserts were added to the Friday menu once a month. To work off the extra calories brought on by the free food, my employer provided plenty of exercise opportunities. The parking lot doubled as a basketball half court, there was a fully equipped exercise room and a ping pong table in the recreation room. At times, it seemed like I wasn't leaving home each morning to go to work; I was going to summer camp.

On one summer afternoon, after a basketball game, I told a friend, "This is as good as it gets." In fact, I went on to say, "I don't think I'll ever leave this company!" It was a very presumptuous thing to say, but that's how I felt. I had been in the desert of employment and now I was enjoying an employment oasis with desserts.

The first year of employment with my latest company went extremely well. I was making a contribution and my efforts were appreciated. As a result, my first performance review yielded a generous merit increase. I was completely satisfied with my new employer and it appeared that the words that I uttered to my friend would become true. But suddenly, a conflict with one of my coworkers began to sour my relationship with the company.

When the conflict between me and the coworker reached the boiling point, I was transferred from the development team to the Quality Assurance (QA) department. While I didn't receive an immediate change in salary, the transfer was clearly a demotion. Like most software companies, my current employer valued their software developers and showed their appreciation by providing generous stock options, state-of-the-art equipment and other special treatment.

The move to QA was a fall from grace. Instead of designing and implementing software solutions, I would now test the software solutions that others had produced. Besides executives and high-level managers, the software developers were at the top of the food chain. I was now on the outside looking in. In short time, my compensation would reflect my new status. Because I could not afford to quit my QA position, with a chip on my shoulder, I accepted my new role within the company.

On the first day in my new role I met Lisa. Lisa had a master's degree in electrical engineering, and she was looking to change careers. After working as a hardware engineer for a number of years, she wanted to become a software engineer. When we discovered that we shared an interest in software development, our friendship deepened. Right away we started thinking about how we could automate our QA tasks by writing software. Within a week, we were able to convince the QA manager to allow us to write a custom software test program.

The program that we began to develop turned out to be my audition for Lisa. We only worked together for a few weeks, before she moved on to another company. But in the brief time that we spent together, I made quite an impression on Lisa. About a month after her departure, I received a phone call from Lisa, informing me that her company was looking for a software engineer to play a key role in the development of a cutting-edge security system.

Our conversation went something like, "Darryl, I've been telling them all about you. You are just what they are looking for. Are you still available?" Lisa stated, before I could get a word in. I had some job prospects, but nothing that compared to the position that Lisa had described. So I sent her my updated resume and, in a few weeks, I was called in for an interview.

When I arrived for the meeting, I was escorted into a room where I was joined by two men, Craig and Cordell. According to Lisa, Craig was the primary decision maker. His decision to hire me over the other candidates would rest on my pending interview.

After Craig kicked off the interview with a question, his phone started ringing. "Excuse me, Darryl, I need to take this call." Craig said with a bit of urgency before asking Cordell to continue the interview in his absence. I never found out who called Craig or what matter required his immediate attention. What I do know is that Craig told Cordell and me that he would return to the interview in a few minutes, but he returned about three hours later.

Immediately after Craig left the room, Cordell's phone started ringing. "Excuse me, Darryl, I need to take this call," he said with a little less urgency in his voice than Craig had displayed. "Yes, sure honey. Okay yes, yes, um okay, okay," replied Cordell to the caller on the other end. After he hung up the phone, I said, "So, I'm assuming that was the boss on the other end of the phone." He chuckled a bit then said, "Well, my wife wants me to come home on time tonight because we're going to a small-group Bible study."

With that revelation, our conversation shifted from the technical interview to a discussion about our spiritual journeys. Although we spoke for about three hours, it seemed like minutes; the time just got away from us. In fact, we never discussed anything that was even remotely technical.

When Craig finally returned to the room, he said, "Darryl, I really apologize for taking so long to return. It looks like I'll need to meet with Cordell and make a decision based on his recommendation." With that, Cordell escorted me out to the lobby. As soon as we got beyond Craig's ear shot, Cordell turned to me and said very discreetly, "Darryl, I'm going to recommend that you get the job. Man, I sure hope you know something about computers!"

Fortunately, I had come a long way from my first IT position. Nevertheless, consistent with the "Darryl Brumfield Story," I concluded an interview for an IT position without answering one IT question. And based on Cordell's recommendation, I was hired.

The new opportunity in front of me trumped my current job in technology, salary, benefits and perks. I was upgraded from a cube to my own office and there was a full-service cafeteria stocked with all my favorite foods and juices. Technically speaking, I was working on the most interesting project that I had ever worked on. The company was associated with an upscale private gym that was a convenient two-minute walk from the office. I cut my commute in half, from 8 miles to 4 miles. Finally, my new employer was in the process of improving their campus, a colorful basketball full court was one of the many improvements.

One day, as I was shooting some baskets after work, I remembered my declaration that my previous job was as good as it gets. My reflection was followed by a burst of laughter. However, my laughter quickly turned into tears of contrition, as my heavenly father gave me the following gentle rebuke.

We can never think it is as good as it gets because with God it can get better. God can always surpass what he has already done. God can do exceedingly above all that we ask or even think! I mistook a plateau for the mountain top.

Although my error manifested itself in my workplace, my correction has benefitted other parts of my life. Our relationships, particularly our relationship with God, can always get deeper. We will never reach the mountain top in this life; we only move from one level to the next level; and we will face valleys in between them.

Whenever we settle and make a plateau a mountain top, we choke our faith, cease to dream and hinder our spiritual growth. We must always remain flexible. We must always maintain a loose grip on the things of this world. Where you are today may not be where God wants you to be tomorrow. Truly, lessons are better caught than taught, and that day, while shooting baskets, I caught the danger of mistaking plateaus for mountain tops.

Still, God knows how much we love our plateaus; he knows that sometimes we need a push to leave them. Sometimes the push comes by way of circumstance, and sometimes that push comes from people. God used a coworker to give me the nudge that I needed, and God used David's brothers to give him the push that he needed.

The day that David caught Saul's attention started like most other days. David wasn't looking to make a career move. However, while visiting his brothers, he overheard someone say that whoever killed Goliath would be able to wed the king's daughter and not pay taxes.[25] This seemed like a good deal, so he asked his brothers about it. They quickly rebuffed and dismissed him, so he asked someone else the same thing. When he inquired about the matter the second time, someone informed the king. With haste, the king sent for David and suddenly David was thrust into the spotlight.

Yes, David seemed to be an ambitious person, certainly his ears perked up when he heard about the prize for killing Goliath. Nevertheless, it's possible that David may have been reluctant to approach the king concerning the matter, so God made the first move. When David was dismissed by his brothers, their brush-off became God's push off.

David began the day satisfied with being one of Israel's greatest shepherds, but God had called him to be

[25] 1 Samuel 17:25-27

one of Israel's greatest kings. The time had come for David to move from his current plateau as a shepherd to a higher one as a king. Sometimes, like David, we need a little help from God to make the transition from one job to the next. That is especially true when we are comfortable in our current job.

Now, I know this may sound somewhat narcissistic, but for the most part, people tend to like me. I couldn't understand why my coworker was so adversarial toward me. Initially, I expended a considerable amount of energy trying to analyze my coworker. I was really upset with the coworker that opposed me and I wanted to know what was driving the opposition. If I knew what was waiting for me on the other side, I would have thanked my coworker for pushing me off my plateau.

David's brothers wanted to rain on David's parade, but he didn't let their attitude defeat him. David turned from them to another, sometimes we need to follow David's example. For me, that meant not quitting but continuing to work hard, even though I received a demotion.

Like David, I had to turn to someone else (Lisa) and bring up the same matter. When the software development department showed me the door, instead of manually testing software for the quality assurance department, I developed a software solution to automate the testing.

In route to accomplishing God's plan we will be helped by some and hindered by others. God will send people in our life to encourage us, but he will also allow us to encounter people who discourage us. In short, God uses haters and celebrators to push us toward our destiny. In the end, they both are God's instruments.

So if someone or something has suddenly threatened your dream job, don't waste time being bitter. Don't invest all of your energy into figuring out their motives. Instead, do what David did. "He then turned away to someone else and brought up the same matter." That is a winning combination. It may not protect your current plateau, but it will prepare you for the next one.

CHAPTER 9

Bait & Fate or the Princess & the Prize

Now the Israelites had been saying, "Do you see how this man keeps coming out? He comes out to defy Israel. The king will give great wealth to the man who kills him. He will also give him his daughter in marriage and will exempt his family from taxes in Israel. David asked the men standing near him, what will be done for the man who kills this Philistine and removes this disgrace from Israel?"[26]

God knows how to motivate us. More often than not, he uses natural impulses as a gateway to supernatural experiences. David had a very natural desire, he wanted to marry the king's daughter and not pay taxes. Let's face it, on the surface David's goal wasn't very spiritual. However, David came to realize that marrying the king's

[26] 1 Samuel 17:25-26

daughter and not paying taxes was nothing more than the means to God's end.

So what was the previous chapter really about? Why did God allow me to enter into a contentious relationship with a coworker? Why did he hijack my interview with Cordell? While I cannot claim to know the mind of God, I am certain of one thing.

I thought the interview with Cordell was God's answer to my latest employment dilemma, nothing more. Like David, I wanted to improve my social economic status; I was chasing the prize. But my shallow perspective did not hinder God's plans. He was up to something. If you pay close attention to the twists and turns that preceded my interview with Cordell, you will find out what he was up to.

About a year before the contention with my coworker reached its feverish peak, with much anguish, I resigned from my position as the lead pastor of an inner-city church. My decision to stop pastoring a church was driven by two primary factors. First, my marriage, which eventually ended during this season of my life, was on the brink of a divorce. Secondly, I made a strategic decision as pastor that did not sit well with the congregation.

Shortly after launching the church, my wife told me that she was overwhelmed by the responsibilities that came with leading a church. In her mind, our marriage was rocky from the beginning and the added responsibility of leading a church would certainly push us over the edge. She was right. I thought our new role as church leaders would stabilize our marriage. So in spite of her, I decided to launch the church. I was wrong.

At first, the charismatic services within the church, service to the outside community and the growing attendance overshadowed our dysfunctional marriage. But over time, the drama in our marriage became so apparent Stevie Wonder could see it. Consequently, the church attendance began to decline. When I shared my vision and strategic plan for the church, a mass exodus ensued.

In a relatively short period of time, the church grew from a handful of people to nearly one hundred. So, for accountability sake, I decided that our congregation needed to affiliate with a larger community of churches.

Without much deliberation with the congregation or the church board, I announced to the congregation that we would affiliate with a predominantly white suburban church movement.

This decision was problematic for a number of reasons. To begin with, I was raised in a predominantly African-American Pentecostal church. My church, the church where I was raised, and where I launched my teaching ministry, was historically affiliated with a highly regarded predominantly African-American denomination. For the most part, the church that I was leading was comprised of people who shared the same background that I had. While I was willing, in the name of racial reconciliation, to break away from my roots, the majority of the congregation were not willing to follow me. Shortly after my announcement, I preached my last message as the senior pastor.

After closing the doors of the church for the last time, I drove from Los Angeles to my home in Orange County. When I reached the mid-way mark, I wept. I remember uttering these words, "Lord, what will happen to me?" The teary-eyed petition was birthed by my utter confusion regarding my future.

I wondered why God planted a seed of racial reconciliation in my heart. In my mind, my obedience to what I thought God led me to do was rewarded with failure. My desire to pastor a multi-ethnic church that was equally diverse in its socio-economic makeup was unsuccessful. It just didn't make sense; I felt I did what God asked me to do and no good thing came from it.

I was in limbo, and I had no idea what my next move would be. Part of me wanted to focus on teaching small groups of people in a home bible study setting; no pulpits, no podiums, no more topical messages. Yet, at the same time, I still had the itch to preach messages in larger venues where I could inspire people to take that next step in faith. I wanted to return to my roots of street evangelism, but at the same time I couldn't shake the desire to equip people within the church by teaching in-depth Bible studies, studies that would provide the framework for whatever they felt God called them to do. I was compelled to start serving in Orange County (OC) but, I was equally compelled to serve in Los Angeles (LA) County.

I was all over the place, in mind and heart. Which move was the right move, urban LA or suburban OC? Equip people in the church by teaching or reach out to people outside the church through preaching evangelistic inspirational messages? Should I walk with a few people at close range or preach to a congregation from a distance? Initially, I chose the path that was most convenient; sit on the sidelines. During that time I visited multiple churches in LA and OC. Since I was carrying the weight of failure, both as a pastor and as a husband, sitting on the sidelines made the most sense.

There are some Bible passages that are often quoted recklessly. One of those passages states that a pastor should have only one wife, and another passage says that a man is not fit for ministry if that man cannot rule his house.[27] I knew these passages, which rightly emphasized the importance of character, were often quoted out of context to disqualify divorced people from

---

[27] 1 Timothy 3:12

church roles like teaching and leadership. Because I was worn down from the marriage and the church, I expediently used the legalistic interpretation of those passages to abandon teaching in churches.

After a brief sabbatical from church altogether, I decided to visit one of the largest churches in OC. I chose this church because I thought that it would be a great place to hide. However, after a Sunday service, as I was heading to my car, I heard someone yell, "Darryl! Darryl!" The voice belonged to the pastor who had encouraged me to affiliate with his predominantly Caucasian suburban church.

When this pastor inquired about the church that I had pastored, I spared him the details but informed him that I was no longer leading a church. He then asked, "Where are you teaching?" I replied "I'm not doing that anymore." He pressed, "Well, what are your future plans?" I answered, "I don't have any plans." With that he said, "I have a great idea," and quickly ushered me into his office.

When I took my seat, I noticed that a large stack of papers were on his desk. For some reason, I asked him about the large stack of papers. He said, "These are applicants who want to teach here. Unfortunately, we only have room for one more class." I noticed that many of the applicants were extremely qualified and even possessed graduate-level seminary training.

I wondered why this pastor, who eventually became one of my mentors and spiritual fathers, invited me into his office. But he ended my speculation when he offered me an opportunity to join his teaching team at their ministry school. Feeling somewhat unqualified because of my lack of formal Bible training, I asked the pastor why he would want me to teach seeing that he had so many other qualified candidates. He replied, "I feel that God wants you to start teaching again, and you might as well start here." So, my self-imposed sabbatical/pity-party from teaching came to an abrupt end, and I found myself teaching Bible studies at one of the largest suburban churches in the country.

At the end of the spring semester, several students approached me and ask if I would lead a Bible study in their home during the summer break. About six months after that, another friend tapped me to lead a second home Bible study in Compton. So now, in addition to teaching at the church, I was teaching two small-group home Bible studies.

The distance between the two groups measured in miles was small, but in just about every other way, the groups were light years apart. One group met in Costa Mesa behind what locals called the "Orange Curtain," a phrase coined to describe an area about halfway between Los Angeles and San Diego where people fled to escape the trappings of urban Los Angeles. The inner-city location of the Compton study embodied everything the OC residents were running away from.

For me, the diversity between the two groups was both a blessing and a burden. Having grown up in Compton, I didn't have many close friendships with non-African-Americans. The Costa Mesa group gave me an opportunity to develop some close relationships with people who didn't look like me. Besides that, this study allowed me to really test what I believed and what I had been teaching others.

Week after week, I would show up to teach in OC, and every week I was not disappointed. The truth of scripture would trump political ideology, culture, ethnicity and everything that opposed it. I was having the time of my life. But, as I traveled up and down the 405 freeway to teach, I was saddened by the grim reality that Sunday morning in America was/is the most segregated day of the week. And while I thoroughly enjoyed teaching at the church in OC, I hungered for a more intentional approach toward reconciliation across ethnic, social and economic lines.

One night Val, a woman who attended the study in Compton, decided to also attend the study in Costa Mesa. After, I finished the teaching for the evening, someone asked her to compare the two groups. Val smiled and said, "Well, I think Darryl is a little more animated at our study in Compton; other than that, there isn't much of a difference." Then, with some hesitation and reservation, she added the following comment, "Besides the fact that I'm the only white person at the Compton study and Darryl is the only black person at this study, the studies are pretty much the same." Although she wasn't attempting to make a joke, her reply made us all laugh.

After we gained our composure, the woman who hosted the Costa Mesa study offered a word of encouragement. Acquainted with my desire to engage in cross-cultural ministry, in a light-hearted way she said, "Darryl, you're teaching black people in Compton and white people in Costa Mesa, maybe before you can get us all in one room together, you need to start teaching Asian people too. You can't leave them out. Maybe that's your problem." I laughed and didn't pay it much mind, until I found myself in the interview with Cordell two weeks later.

Cordell, who just happened to be African-American, mentioned that Asian-Americans comprised the predominant ethnicity of his church and his small group. When he said that, I paused for a moment and said to myself, "Okay God, what are you up too?"

My reaction to Cordell's statement was prompted by the conversation that I had with a woman after a home Bible study just two weeks earlier. Was it a coincidence that Cordell attended a church that was comprised of mainly Asian-Americans? Was there a connection between that light-hearted conversation and the interview?

For the next three hours Cordell and I talked about his church and its lead pastor, Dave. Time and time again, I would share my views regarding cross cultural ministry with Cordell and he would respond, "That's what Dave says all the time." By the end of the interview, I knew more about Cordell's church than the position for which I was interviewing.

Cordell's church was located in the city of Irvine. According to several publications, it was the safest city in America. However, under Dave's leadership, the church wasn't looking to play it safe. From day one, Dave challenged his congregation to radically love their neighbor. A pretty mild idea, until you understand the biblical meaning of the word neighbor.

Your neighbor, according to Jesus, isn't only someone who lives next door to you. Most likely, your neighbor is someone who may live on the other side of town or the other side of the world. Consequently, more often than not, your neighbor won't share your political views, your social customs or your traditions. And when that is the case, because of where it can take you, loving your neighbor can become messy and even dangerous.

Without my knowledge, God was using my trials to prepare me for a season of service at this messy, dangerous church. My pain had purpose; the seeds of reconciliation that were planted while I was leading my small church in Compton had equipped me to serve at this messy place. Because of my relationship with Cordell, I eventually joined his church family. Dave, the founding pastor of my new church home, became one of my closest friends.

Through my relationship with Dave, I have met some really cool neighbors as I traveled the world sharing the good news in diverse settings. It's been quite a ride. Sometimes I'm in a suburban warehouse speaking to large audiences and sometimes in a room with just a few people. On any given Friday night, you might find me sharing the good news with my neighbors on a street corner in downtown Los Angeles' Skid Row. I have engaged my neighbors in a coffee shop in Bangkok, Thailand. I've met with my neighbors in a London pub and I've connected with my neighbors in Southeast Asia in remote villages under a tin roof.

The space and place are really secondary; it's about magic that happens there. And in every space and in every place, the majesty of God's truth and love always trumps the superficial differences that exist between the people in the room or hut. But how does my connection to a church that seeks to love its neighbors connect with David and his classic confrontation with Goliath?

David didn't seek to become king. All he wanted was to marry the princess and avoid taxes; all I wanted was a job. But God wanted more for David and for me than we wanted for ourselves. David's story was bigger than marrying a princess, and "The Darryl Brumfield Story" is bigger than landing jobs with perks. In the end, my most recent job transition, like all my other employment transitions, wasn't about IT. The perks may have provided bait, but that's all.

God was not orchestrating the events behind the scenes to bring me to a place of comfort for comfort's sake. He strategically placed me in the IT field and he was navigating my career in that field for a greater purpose than I could have ever envisioned. When I sat down for the first IT interview of my career, God knew that it would eventually lead to my interview with Cordell. God was setting his plan in motion, a plan that included serving my neighbors around the world.

Yes, God guides our path and orders or steps. He points us in a certain direction; that's what guiding is about. And yes, he uses bait to guide us, but he also orders our steps. That activity requires a little more precision. In my case, choosing technology as a profession was the result of his guiding. But all of the doors that opened and closed for me in IT were the result of God ordering my steps with precision!

The sudden change in favor with my previous employer, the timing of my work with Lisa, Lisa's job change, and her recommendation that I join her team were not coincidental. God ordained my meeting with Cordell and knew it would lead to a fruitful season of service. He is doing that in your life as well. He's making moves. Maybe it's time for you to acknowledge God's sovereign direction.

No matter what juncture you are in your career, never forget that your profession is much bigger than a paycheck and prestige. It's never about the princess and the tax bracket. David might have thought that it was about that, and maybe you think that as well. But your career is bigger than your material compensation.

Every career has some sort of fringe benefit that can be exploited for God's kingdom. Some careers give you access to people, some careers offer flexible schedules, and some allow you to work from anywhere in the world, thus, allowing you to spread the "Good News" of God's grace in Christ to the whole world.

God has strategically placed you where you are today. Embrace your place; know that the events that have shaped you have shaped you for a purpose. I would need to write another book to convey the fruit that came from my interview with Cordell. But know this, the interview occurred at a perfect time in my life—a time when God was beginning to give me clarity on how he wanted to use me to serve him.

On that teary-eyed drive on the 405 freeway, I was so troubled. I was desperately trying to solve a multiple-choice question. In my limited understanding, I was trying to choose between A, B, C and D. But when God gave me insight into my career choice, I discovered that the answer was all of the above, and much more.

As you reflect on your career, do you see God's fingerprints? Have you acknowledged that God is guiding your path and ordering your steps? If so, it's time that you move beyond the bait and begin to kiss your fate.

CHAPTER 10

Favor, Faithfulness & Shepherding

But David said to Saul, "Your servant has been keeping his father's sheep."[28]

After Lisa and I, along with a team of Ph.D.'s and engineers, completed my inaugural project for my new employer, I was faced with another employment challenge. My team and I had successfully developed a state-of-the-art Facial Recognition Security System (FRSS). But there was one problem; our system required users to have a laser scan their face. It turns out, no matter how much you reassure people that a laser is harmless, most people don't want their mug scanned by a

---

[28] 1 Samuel 17:34

laser. Consequently, based on poor pre-market research, our project was shelved.

Six months passed before the (FRSS) project was officially terminated. And because it was touch and go until the project was finally laid to rest, the company did not want the core team to move on to another project. So, for the most part, after successfully launching a pilot installation of the FRSS system, I spent the next six months on a paid sabbatical.

About three of six months was spent on an assignment based in Minnesota. The company sent my team there to provide assistance, if needed. However, the team in Minnesota didn't really need our help, so I spent about three months in Minnesota enjoying its lakes. Sometimes I would just walk around a lake and sometimes I would rent a boat and lay back and enjoy the sun. I was in Minnesota, an extremely cold place characterized by severe winters and intense rainfalls. Yet there I was, Tuesday through Friday and maybe one weekend per month, soaking up the sun and enjoying a sabbatical.

At the end of my God-orchestrated sabbatical, not like the faithless one I coveted many years earlier, it was time to move on. The Internet had created a paradigm shift, and I needed to acquaint myself with the new emerging Web-based software development technologies. But how would I learn this new technology?

In a perfect world, I could maintain my senior salary and learn on the job. But there were no opportunities to develop Internet applications with my current employer. I thought about picking up the Web-development skills in my spare time, but I really didn't have a lot of spare time. In addition to teaching home Bible studies during the week, I was speaking at church on Sunday pretty regularly. I was also mentoring some people at close range during the week. Besides, I would need real-world experience to command my current salary.

One morning, as I sat in my office trying to figure out how I could transition into Internet software development, I received a phone call from an old friend, Tim. He and I had not spoken to each other for more than a year, but he was calling to give me his contact information and to arrange a lunch so that we could catch up. In the course of our conversation, I revealed my aspiration to learn how to develop Internet applications. When I expressed what I saw as my obstacles in achieving a smooth transition, he laughed.

"Darryl, I run an internet consulting company. Why don't you come and work with me. We can pay you 10 percent more than what you are making now and you will get stock options too." I replied, "Tim, I don't have any experience developing internet applications." He quickly responded, "Well, you can learn on the job. I'm confident that you won't have any problem picking up this new technology. And, at the end of one year, I'll give you a 20 percent increase in salary!" Well, my dilemma was solved, and I made another job.

On many fronts, the first nine months of employment with my new company could not have been better scripted. I was quickly learning how to develop Internet applications on two competing technology platforms. The company's valuation was climbing and a successful IPO was eminent.

Because of the potentially lucrative stock options, my coworkers were always in a great mood. A successful IPO would make some people instant millionaires, but everybody would make a substantial amount of money. Nevertheless, one of the best parts of the job for me wasn't my pending stock windfall. For me, reuniting with my hilariously gracious friend was the best part of the job.

Tim would often stop by my desk, smile and then ask this question, "Darryl, are you happy?" If we shared an elevator, he would say, "Darryl, are you happy?" If we were sitting next to each other on a plane, he would say, "Darryl, are you happy?" It became a running joke between us. He would say, "Darryl, are you happy?," and I would laugh and reply, "Yeah man, I'm happy." And whenever I had a speaking engagement and my projects were on schedule, Tim would say, "Darryl, what are you doing here? Shouldn't you be at the beach, reading your Bible and preparing for Sunday?"

All was well; I was having fun learning a new technology. I was on track for the largest payday of my life. I had plenty of time to listen to God. But suddenly, in the tenth month of employment, the Internet bubble popped and the company began to feel the effects.

For the most part, IT had always been a growth profession. However, the industry was entering an era of pronounced contraction. Internet companies were closing their doors on a daily basis. Consequently, the once profitable consulting business of my employer dried up. The joyful buzz regarding the company's pending IPO was replaced with tension over the company's pending layoffs. So when I entered Tim's office to discuss my annual salary review, I had very low expectations.

Taking my seat, I noticed that Tim was extremely uncomfortable about something. When he addressed me, he quickly confirmed my suspicions. "Darryl, I really feel bad about this, really bad. I can't give you the 20 percent increase in salary that I promised you." Thinking I was just about to be canned, I breathed a sigh of relief before I said, "Tim, don't worry about it. No one can predict the future. Hopefully, things will turn around."

Suddenly, Tim smiled and his demeanor changed. He was beaming with excitement from the inside out and he couldn't wait to share his revelation with me. "Darryl,

I got it! I know how I can give you a 20 percent raise! You can work 20 percent less for the same salary." So during the worse down turn in the history of IT, I worked part-time with full salary and benefits. The experience reminded me of an incident that occurred while I was working for my previous employer.

On one of my visits to a lake in Minnesota, as I reading in the park, a perfect stranger approached me and said "Do you know that you are enjoying the best weather we have had all year?" Then he left as quickly as he came. Though he was there for a moment, I sensed that his words would remain with me for much longer. God carved out some sunshine for me in a place known for icy winters. His words were a fitting precursor to what I was now experiencing with my new employer. The words of the gentleman from Minnesota rang true; God had provided sunshine for me in place of icy winters.

I continued to work for Tim until the doors were practically closed. Cutting to the chase, the company would lay off anyone that wasn't on a billable project. Since I could lead a project, develop software or give presentations, Tim had the flexibility to plug me into just about any scenario to ensure my employment. As our client base declined, Tim would switch me from one project to another to make sure I wouldn't get laid off. Every time one of my projects would begin to wind down, Tim would assign me to another project. It was like we were playing musical chairs with projects, until there were no more projects in play.

When I think back on this season of employment, two things come to mind. First, I am moved by God's favor and faithfulness in a time of famine. The job market was grim, but God was gracious and he graciously met all of my needs. Secondly, the experience gave me a window into God's scope and stewardship of time. Unlike you and me, God sees the end from the beginning. Moreover, he decides who we will encounter as we pass through the corridors of time, all with his grand plan in mind.

You see, many years earlier, while working in my first full-time IT role, I became a project manager and Tim just happened to be one of my team members. Tim was extremely ambitious. A recent college graduate, Tim was determined to quickly ascend the corporate ladder.

He was the first person to come to work and he was the last person to leave the office. Eventually, I could not delegate enough work for Tim, so he volunteered to work closer with me on some of my tasks. At the time, I was the lead pastor of a growing church, so I graciously granted his request.

I knew that if we worked together, Tim would help me squeeze a few more hours out of my day— precious hours that I really needed to handle the administrative duties that accompanied a growing congregation. As Tim and I worked together, we became friends. And early one morning, as we were just settling into work, Tim received a phone call that tested the strength of our friendship.

After receiving the phone call, Tim approached me. He was visibly shaken, yet poised at the same time. Fighting through the grief, he said, "Darryl, I have to leave now." I knew that whatever he talked about on the phone had rocked his world. Desiring to reach out to him, I said, "Tim, do you need to talk to someone?"

In a deliberate and solemn voice, he looked at me and said, "Darryl, my sister's boyfriend has beaten her for the last time. I'm going home. I'm going to get my gun, and I'm going to shoot him." After he said that, I persuaded Tim to sit down and discuss his decision with me.

During the course of our friendship, I discovered that Tim, an Asian-American, was the oldest son in his family. I knew that because of his culture and his pecking order in the family, he shouldered a lot of responsibility for his parents. Armed with an understanding of his respect for his parents, I leveraged his parents as I began to counsel him with these words.

"Tim, think about your parents. What will happen to them when you go to jail?" I also pointed out that, while he would be sitting in jail, his sister would continue to engage in abusive relationships. After talking it out, I was able to encourage Tim to have an intervention for his sister at his house.

The drama of that hour laid the ground work for our friendship, a friendship that continued to grow, as we met once a week for Bible study. My friendship with Tim provides both the backdrop for the job story that I shared in this chapter and its most important takeaway.

Simply stated, God decides who we will encounter in this life, but he allows us to decide how we will respond to those people we encounter. We can be so concerned with our own peril that we miss the opportunity to impact the people that God has set before us.

When Tim was distraught over the abuse inflicted on his sister, I had a choice to make. I could meet him in his pain or I could ignore his agony, put my head down and keep working. By choosing to draw Tim out and walk with him in his dark night, God spared Tim and his family from more pain and sorrow. But because God is God, he also allowed me to participate in my own deliverance, which happened many years later during the worst employment season in the history of IT.

Like David, I was simply acting as a shepherd. When I intervened in Tim's personal affairs, I was keeping my father's sheep. Moreover, as I focused on the task at hand, God protected me from the lions and the bears and God knows what else. The kindness that God extended to me exceeded the kindness that I extended to Tim. By the way, many years later, after our season of playing musical chairs with IT projects, Tim became a follower of Jesus at an Easter service. I walked with him as he went forward and declared his faith in Jesus.

Though the employment outlook may be bleak, don't lose heart. God can provide for you in the lean times. Don't look down, look up and then look around you. Look up to God who is able to masterfully orchestrate your deliverance. But also look around you and consider how you might help the casualties of an economic meltdown. From your place of pain, help someone cope with their pain. The person that you help may not be able to offer you a job in the future, but you will experience God in the present.

CHAPTER 11

Employment or Deployment

And Samuel said to Jesse "Are all the young men here?" Then he said "there remains yet the youngest, and there he is, keeping the sheep" ...Then the men of Judah came, and there they anointed David King over the house of Judah... So David reigned over all Israel; and administered judgment and justice to all his people.[29]

When we are so focused on employment or unemployment, we often miss the big picture. As much as it is possible, God wants us to see this world through his lens. But what does it look like to see employment through God's lens? I brushed up against that question in

---

[29] 1 Samuel 16:11; 2 Samuel 2:4; 2 Samuel 8:15

the last chapter; however, I want to take up that question in more detail in this chapter.

When Tim and I could no longer play musical chairs with projects, I was finally laid off. Although I was unemployed for almost four months, I experienced very little anxiety. I knew that God would eventually open a door that no one could close. So instead of sitting around the house thinking about what I couldn't control, I decided to spend some down time at the beach.

I love to look out at the ocean. There is something very majestic about watching the waves come in and roll back out; there is order to it. The tide can only consume a fixed amount of the shore and no more. When I ponder the waves, as they kiss the shoreline, I am reminded that the waves mirror the troubles in life. The waves are controlled by many fine-tuned factors that God put in place, and so are our trials.

As I would sit there on the beach, often waiting for callbacks for interviews, I knew that there was a possibility that I could lose some of my material possessions, but I could not lose anything that truly mattered. Sometimes, while pondering God's masterful design that governs the sea, I would just burst into laughter. The thought of God's ability to control the tide on the beach in front of me and the tide of uncertainty in my life was strangely amusing.

One day as I was contemplating making some financial moves that would stretch my savings, I received a phone call from a recruiter informing me that a company in Los Angeles was interested in my services. However, before an interview could be arranged, I needed to assure the recruiter that I would be willing to make the 55-mile one way commute from Orange County or relocate to LA County. Seeing that I didn't have any job prospects and was burning through my savings account, I instructed the recruiter to set up an interview.

My interview went great, and immediately afterward the Company offered me a job. I was given two weeks to decline or accept their offer. Although I dreaded the commute from my home in South Orange County to a company near the Los Angeles International airport, I breathed a sigh of relief knowing that I would soon have a revenue stream.

Before returning to my car to make the long haul back to Orange County (OC), I spoke to an employee of the company in the break room. The employee just happened to live a few miles from my house in OC. As he was pouring coffee into his cup, he mentioned rather unconvincingly that the commute from OC to LA wasn't that bad. However, his posture and his countenance gave me the impression that he wasn't engaging me to pass on some valuable information. No, he was giving himself a much-needed pep talk.

He reminded me of people who move to Texas and tell you that it's not that hot in summer or people who move to Chicago and tell you that it's not that cold in the winter. He went on to say that if you leave at 4 a.m. you can get here by 5:30 a.m. Unaware of the sigh in his voice and without any enthusiasm, he placed his dinner in the refrigerator and said, "Yeah, it's not that bad. To avoid the rush hour traffic, you can eat dinner here and watch TV in the break room. After 7 p.m. there is hardly any traffic."

As I made my way to my car I began to think about how this job might impact my life outside of work.

Specifically, I wondered how the commute would affect the Bible study that I was teaching in LA and my participation at NEWSONG Church in OC. Concerned about my time management, I thought maybe I could use the commute to listen to Bible studies. But that scenario left me uneasy; there really isn't a substitute for focused quality downtime with God. As I continued to contemplate commuting or relocating, I became restless and puzzled. The best remedy for my agitation was to pray about the situation. My prayer went something like this.

"Father, I thank you for this opportunity and, if you want me to work here, I'm willing to relocate to LA. I'm willing to commute, but I prefer to work in OC. If my desire is in alignment with your plans, I ask that you give me a job in OC."

After my prayer, I felt like I was given the gift of faith. I had no anxiety and was confident that I was in the favor of God's will. The commute didn't matter anymore, my reluctance to relocate didn't matter either. Although I desired what made me comfortable, I was equally willing to forsake comfort, if my comfort hindered God's purposes for me.

When I returned home, I played my answering machine and discovered that a company in Santa Ana (about 20 miles from my home) wanted to interview me. I met with the hiring manager of that company the next day. The interview went extremely well and a job offer followed.

Now, as I was driving home from the interview, I remembered the prayer that I uttered in the parking lot in LA a day earlier, the recollection triggered a smile. Then, without any hesitation and with a little tongue in cheek, I brought another petition to my incredibly gracious God.

"Father, I thank you for this new opportunity that is much closer to my house, one-third of the commute of the previous opportunity. If this opportunity is in line with your plans, I want it. However, if there is another opportunity closer to home, then please give me that job." You see, over time I learned that God has a great sense of humor and that sometime he invites us to experience him in this way.

After I prayed that prayer, I burst into laughter, knowing that my petition was under consideration. When I returned home, I immediately rushed to the answering machine. And what happened a day earlier was repeated again. A company that I had interviewed with a month earlier wanted me to come in for a third interview. This company was in Irvine (about 10 miles from my home).

The company in Irvine wanted me to come in that day to discuss my role and salary. I rushed over to their office right away. The meeting was fruitful and I left with another job offer. By the way, each job offer exceeded the other in both salary and benefits.

As I was driving home from the potential Irvine employer, I felt God saying to me, let's try this one more time. I sensed him wooing me to experience his hilariously generous favor. So once again, beaming with confidence, I offered up the following petition.

"Okay Father, I know that it's nothing for you to give me a job even closer to my house than Irvine, closer than 10 miles from my house. If working closer to home will make me more productive for you, if working closer to home is in harmony with your plans for me, I ask you to open up an opportunity for me closer to home."

When I returned home, I rushed to the phone again. And, as I anticipated, I discovered that the answering machine light was blinking. The message that was recorded on the answering machine was from a recruiter named Thomas. He worked for a company that was about 4 miles from my home.

Before I returned Thomas's phone call, I took a minute to reflect on the past couple of days. At the beginning of the week, I had no offers on the table. Now I had three offers and possibly a fourth. But again, I cannot underscore this enough; it's never about getting a job. God can always give us more jobs than we can receive; he's God. So, in this instance, what was my journey from one job to another really about?

After some prayer and reflection, I returned Thomas's phone call. I expected to reach his voicemail because it was late in the evening, but to my surprise, Thomas answered my call with great enthusiasm. "Darryl, Darryl Brumfield, I was hoping you would call me tonight!" he blurted out the minute I told him my name.

It turns out that Thomas was a college roommate of Tim, my friend and previous gracious employer. Thomas had lost Tim's contact information and noticed that I had listed Tim as a reference. Although the position that I had applied for required a master's degree (remember I had no degree), because I reunited Thomas with his college roommate he decided to highly recommend me for the job. Moreover, he requested that the hiring manager expedite his interview process for me because I had pending offers. The manager complied, and one week later I was hired.

On my first day of work, I was told that I just needed to make sure that my workstation, e-mail and network access rights were correct, then head up stairs to complete my employee orientation. The plan was to take it easy for the first day and then be ready to start my first assignment on the following day.

But my first assignment could not wait until the next day; it required my immediate attention. After I confirmed that my working environment was in order, I headed upstairs to meet with Human Resources and begin my orientation. When I arrived for my orientation,

I was greeted by Thomas, who showed me the facilities before escorting me into his office. After taking his seat and mechanically reviewing the Company benefits, Thomas unexpectedly stopped speaking and started sobbing.

After about twenty seconds Thomas, who had placed his head on his desk, lifted up his head and apologized for allowing his emotions to get the best of him. I assured him that I wasn't offended and asked him if he would like to discuss what was bothering him. After some hesitation, Thomas took me up on my offer.

Wiping away his tears he said, "Darryl, I'm going through a divorce. The divorce has been brutal on me and my children (most divorces are) and I now feel like I'm disqualified from ministry because of it."

Suddenly, I understood why God shortened my commute. Thomas and I had a lot in common. The circumstances of Thomas's divorce were similar to the circumstances in my own divorce. The fears that Thomas had regarding his children were not foreign to me. But most of all, I understood how divorce can make one feel like an outcast in church. Thomas felt that he was disqualified from a public ministry, like teaching and I understood where he was coming from.

I spent the rest of the day in Thomas' office. At one point during our fruitful five-hour dialog, Thomas shared that he was leading a Bible study of about thirty people and how he now felt disqualified to lead. Because of his pending divorce, he felt that his opportunity to serve as a teacher was now lost.

I told Thomas my marriage failed in front of a much larger audience, but God didn't write me off and that God wouldn't write him off either. How comforting it was to see the burden lift from Thomas when, in the process of sharing my journey, Thomas learned that my marriage failed in front of hundreds but God still used me to speak to thousands after that.

When most people think about God's holiness they tend to associate God's holiness with things that people don't do or things people don't wear or places people don't go. In short, they feel that they are practicing holiness by not doing certain things. Unfortunately, to reduce God's holiness to a list of do's and a larger list of don'ts, is to miss the meaning of God's holiness.

God's holiness is related to God's "otherness." God is not like others. God is unique and his ways are unique. The creator is different than his creation and greater than anything that one might imagine. Thomas and I celebrated God's "otherness," and we rejoiced that God is not like men. It's liberating to know that God doesn't write people off! God can use us in spite of or sometimes in light of our failures.

Two weeks later Thomas stopped by my desk to thank me for my counsel and to inform me that he was leaving the company. I was encouraged to hear him say that he believed God could use him to teach others again. Moreover, he didn't care how large or how small his next assignment would be. In the end, numbers don't really matter. What does matter, and what I saw in Thomas, was his willingness and desire to accept God's next assignment for him. No matter the size.

As we were saying our goodbyes, Thomas said that our meeting was a divine appointment; I agreed. You see, Thomas had planned to leave the company around the same time that I was laid off from my previous employer. For about four months he was trying to make a transition; however, he was unable to make it happen. We both felt that his delayed departure and my delayed arrival were not a coincidence.

My career and yours is about deployment not employment. Our careers are much like King David's. David was deployed into the fields to care for sheep, David was deployed to the battlefields to lead Israel into victory and he was deployed to the office of king to raise Israel to its zenith in history. David was either actively deployed or God was preparing him for his next deployment.

For the most part, with exception to providing the backdrop that cemented my friendship with Tim, I have focused on the transition from one company to another. But my deployments are more important than my transition from one job to the next one.

On September 11, 2001, I happened to be deployed in a high-rise office building. A day after the towers fell, a woman representing the leasing office of that building approached me. She said, "I heard you were a minister. Would you mind leading a memorial service for the tenants?"

For weeks after the memorial service, the elevator became my counseling booth. People would comment on the memorial service that we had in the courtyard and then launch into issues that they were facing. September 11 was a wakeup call. Although it didn't last long, the tragic event made people consider their mortality and the deeper questions of life. God deployed me to that company for that season to help some people with the questions with which they were wresting.

If the transition from one job to the next one is taking longer than you think it should, try to see employment and unemployment through God's lens. If you do that, you will be able to rest in God's wisdom. Moreover, you will be able to take comfort in knowing that God has not forgotten about you. His divine delays have purpose. Sometimes God is preparing our hearts for the next deployment and sometimes he's preparing the hearts of those who we will encounter when we are deployed.

CHAPTER 12

Pride & Providence

Then Nathan said to David, "You are the man! This is what the LORD, the God of Israel, says: "I anointed you king over Israel, and I delivered you from the hand of Saul. I gave your master's house to you, and your master's wives into your arms. I gave you the house of Israel and Judah. And if all this had been too little, I would have given you even more. Why did you despise the word of the LORD by doing what is evil in his eyes? You struck down Uriah the Hittite with the sword and took his wife to be your own.[30]

As I stated in the previous chapter, after a season of unemployment, God began to open doors for me. One of the doors that opened belonged to a very reputable company in Santa Ana, California. The board

---

[30] 2 Samuel 12:7-9

room of this company serves as the back drop for my next job story. It's where God took me to task and reminded me of another truth that transcends employment. The truth that was reinforced that day still impacts my life and I hope it will have an impact on yours.

After I concluded a successful interview with Ken, the Software Development Manager, he expressed his interest to make me an offer. However, when he made the offer a day later, I already had two other offers to consider. Committed to bringing me on board, he was able to sway the company to increase my starting salary, making it competitive with my other offers. But before the offer could be made official, I needed to interview with the executive team. The team included two vice presidents and two directors.

I arrived at the company for my second interview beaming with confidence and self-assurance; I was on top of the world. God was moving at light speed. After many months of unemployment, I now had three job offers on the table. But because God had moved so swiftly, my heart was filled with pride. In fact, when I entered the conference room for my final interview, I felt like I was doing them a favor by gracing them with my presence.

With one exception, Ken and the executive team were very cordial. Frank, the one exception, was very cold and hard. Nevertheless, because God used Frank in a tremendous way, it's Frank who I am most grateful for today. Unlike the other participants, Frank entered the room with a very stern look on his face; no smiles, all business. After taking their seats, one by one the executive team began to ask me questions about my work history.

As I talked about my work history, Ken would smile and casually look over at the other team members as if to say, "I told you so, show him the money!" But there was a problem brewing; the more I talked about my accomplishments, the more my pride began to swell. I felt large and in charge. So with Frank's help, God provided an attitude adjustment.

After I concluded recounting my work history, Frank decided that it was his turn to take me down memory lane; however, he didn't want to take the scenic route. Frank, in a very harsh and unapologetic voice said,

"So Darryl, I see here that you went to UCI, but you did not finish your degree. So the last school that you graduated from was your high school in Compton, correct?"

Somehow, Frank knew that not having a degree was a sore spot for me. Having pierced my thin veil of confidence, like a shark attracted to blood in the water, Frank continued to shred my confidence with a host questions. "Darryl, I see here that you were laid off from your third job after a few months." Before I could answer, he quickly asked another question.

I was in the hot seat and Frank was turning up the heat. With distain in his voice, Frank began to pick my resume apart, as he emphasized my lack of education. But, about midway through Frank's tirade, something very magical happened; suddenly I was reminded of God's favor. Overcome by God's kindness and faithfulness toward me, I was moved to repentance. The experience was so surreal that Frank's voice seemed to fade into the background.

I came into that interview like a huge ship, pulling into a harbor in its entire splendor, but Frank's deconstruction of my career broke my ship into little pieces of plank. Yes, I had multiple job offers on the table, but I made it to shore on broken pieces of the ship that had crashed upon the rocks of hard knocks.

I wasn't an ideal candidate for admission to UCI. I did get married at an early age and, as a result, left college before completing my degree. I wasn't the most qualified applicant for many of the positions that I had held. And on a personal level, I had endured some major relational setbacks, like the sting of divorce and the emotional and financial shockwaves that follow that kind of a life change.

I was not a big, grand ship pulling into the harbor. Nevertheless, because of God, I had made it to shore on broken pieces of the ship. As this revelation sunk in, with Frank's voice faintly echoing in the background, I released my pride, I clung to God and began to rejoice in God's power. As Frank continued to review my work history, undercutting every job that I ever held, I would get lost in the story behind the job.

When Frank mentioned my less than grandiose exit from UCI, I thought about my last visit with my UCI academic counselor. In that interview, my academic counselor, seeking to help me out, suggested that I pursue a non-technical career. She said a hard science would be too difficult for someone with my background, someone who showed up late to the booming IT-career party. She said that people who major in hard sciences or technical fields like engineering show an aptitude for it early in life. But because I knew God, her counsel didn't discourage me, it only made me more determined.

I knew that God would prove her wrong, and in time he did. In fact, later in my career I worked side by side with her husband (a brilliant engineer) at one of my jobs, before he was laid off. So as I began to think about the many stories behind the story, Frank became somewhat of a softball praise pitcher. He would lob me memories that I would hit out the park and rejoice in God's faithfulness, as I rounded the bases.

When Frank began to conclude his assessment of my credentials and work history, I began to slowly fade back into the interview at hand. I didn't want to leave the praise party that I was having, refocusing on the interview was a difficult task. I was anxious for the interview to be over. I wanted to escape to my car and praise God in private.

I wanted to be all alone in my car, just me and God having fun and fellowship; just me and him reminiscing about his exploits. How he did much with little and always manifested himself when I really needed him too. The interview for me was now secondary; my attitude adjustment was the primary thing. Nevertheless, I did have an interview to finish, but how could I finish strong?

The climate in the room had gone from cordial to hostile in a matter of minutes. You could hear a pen drop and everyone was clearly uncomfortable and tensed. But, thanks to God's sense of humor, the interview did finish on a high and hilarious note.

Frank, confident that he had convinced his colleagues that I was not qualified for the position, ended his verbal assault with one final question. With a bit of crudeness in his voice, Frank said, "If you were hired, you would lead a team of developers that have bachelor's degrees, some of the developers have master's degrees. Darryl, you don't have any formal training in project management. You don't even have a college degree. How would you feel leading a team of people who have at least a bachelor's degree? How would you feel working with this team, we all have master's degrees?"

After he uttered those words, the room was silent for about a second, though the awkward silence made it seem much longer. Then, composed and refreshed from my praise party, I leaned back in my chair, smiled and said very confidently with bit of sarcasm "Well Frank, to tell you the truth, I haven't given it much thought. But since you bring it up now, as I consider how I would feel about working with people who hold master's degrees, I think I would feel the same way I felt when I managed and worked with people that held doctorate degrees."

With my response to Frank's question, the room erupted in laughter. Ken was doubled over in his seat, the directors and the vice presidents did a better job concealing their emotion, each covering their mouth with their hand as they laughed. Their restraint seemed to be aimed at Frank, the only person in the room who did not find my answer the least bit amusing. Still, even Frank seemed to force a smile, though he remained silent for the rest of the interview, which did conclude on a very high note. The next day Ken called to extend a job offer.

Although I respectfully declined the offer, I devoted a chapter to this interview because of the importance of the truth that the story underpins. As I stated, the lesson that was reinforced that day transcends the business realm. Simply stated, Frank reminded me of the beauty of God's favor and the folly of our pride.

Pride is a very dangerous thing because it fosters self-reliance. Pride, birthed and fed on our achievements, often causes us to either factor God out altogether or transform him into our tool. Either way, in our own eyes, we become more than whom we are and God becomes less than who he is. Yet, because unemployment can damage one's self-esteem, seeking to heal a bruised ego, many people are turning to resources that prop up their self-image. Unfortunately, some of the self-help materials being peddled are doing more harm than good.

Sadly, we value self-reliance, and we heap praises on those who are filled with self-confidence. I was becoming one of those people, but God would not let that happen. Whenever we are encouraged to trust in our ability, our wit, our money, our education or anything other than God, we are in a dangerous place.

Conventional wisdom suggests that we derive our strength from self-confidence, as we feed our ego with our achievements. Most self-help books today promote your inner self. And, at the end of the day, they want you to put your faith in yourself. But is that God's way? Does God want us to be fuelled by self-confidence? I think not.

David was the beneficiary of God's grace, but over time pride got the best of him. Pride gave him a sense of entitlement and, filled with that sense of entitlement, David took another man's wife for his own. Moreover, to cover up his sin, he had the woman's husband killed.[31] Pride took David to a place that he never thought he would go.

But God loved David, and because God loved David, he sent Nathan to give David a much-needed reality check.[32] King David forgot about his humble beginnings. He needed to be reminded that the coveted

---

[31] 2 Samuel 11:3-24
[32] 2 Samuel 12:1

and highly respected position he now held was not solely a result of his own doing. Yes, he had the courage to face a lion, a bear and even a giant. But his success was more about God's power than David's perseverance.

What is true of David is true of everyone who achieves a measure of success. There really aren't any self-made millionaires, though many boast of their work ethic and how they achieved success by applying themselves. They will tell you how they worked harder and worked smarter than others. But the truth is, there are people who are twice as smart and work twice as hard who have never made more than $2 a day. It's God who gives us our health and our opportunities.

King David's head was in the clouds, his humility was gone. But after Nathan spoke to him, David realized his error. Although his intensions may not have been pure and though he didn't know that he was God's servant, Frank was my Nathan. God used Frank to give me a reality check and I am eternally grateful for it.

I encourage you to perform a little exercise. Take a trip down memory lane, but don't take the scenic route. Take the route that amplifies God's grace in your life.

Take the route that fills you with gratitude instead of pride. That trip will serve you well, and it will end with a praise party.

CHAPTER 13

Encouragement or Empowerment

*Then King David went in and sat before the Lord, and he said:
"Who am I, Sovereign Lord, and what is my family, that you
have brought me this far? And as if this were not enough in your
sight, Sovereign Lord, you have also spoken about the future of
the house of your servant—and this decree, Sovereign Lord, is for
a mere human! "What more can David say to you? For you
know your servant, Sovereign Lord. For the sake of your word
and according to your will, you have done this great thing and
made it known to your servant.*

*"How great you are, Sovereign Lord! There is no one like you,
and there is no God but you, as we have heard with our own
ears. And who is like your people Israel—the one nation on
earth that God went out to redeem as a people for himself, and to
make a name for himself, and to perform great and awesome
wonders by driving out nations and their gods from before your
people, whom you redeemed from Egypt? You have established
your people Israel as your very own forever, and you, Lord, have
become their God.*[33]

---

[33] 2 Samuel 7:18-24 NIV

My Dad's side of the family pumped out preachers like Detroit pumps out Chryslers. My father had seven siblings and just about all of his siblings had at least one son that stood behind a podium on Sunday mornings. Consequently, when the time came for my Aunt Sylvia's eulogy, we were not short-handed. One by one, my cousins took the podium. And one by one, they all stole my opening. All of my cousins thought that they were Aunt Sylvia's favorite nephew. Clearly, like my God, my Aunt Sylvia, who we all called "Ant-Tee," knew how to make all of us feel special.

The Apostle John could relate to me and my cousins, he knew what it meant to feel like you are favored. When, I read the Gospel of John for the first time, I was puzzled by this phrase "the Disciple who Jesus loved."[34] The phrase troubled me because it seemed to suggest that Jesus loved this one disciple more than he loved the others. After some investigation, I discovered that John, the author of The Gospel of John, used that phrase to refer to himself. Although Jesus loved everyone, John wanted everyone to know that Jesus had a

[34] John 13:23

special love for him. To know that you are loved in a very unique way is something that we all covet, especially when that love comes from a father.

When my children were young, I would tuck them into bed in the following manner. First, I would go into my daughter's room. She would say, "Dad, tell me a story." Now I always told a rendition of the same story, a story about the fictitious kingdom of "Brumfield-Dom."

In kingdom of "Brumfield-Dom," the princess, who happened to have the same name as my daughter, would always find herself in some type of peril. But by the end of the story, the princess would be rescued by her king. Sometimes the king would slay a dragon, sometimes he would fight giants, but he would always prevail and rescue the princess. Of course, the king was an extension of me. After her bedtime story, my daughter, without a care in the world, would close her eyes and drift off to sleep.

After my daughter closed her eyes, I would immediately enter my son's room and began our nightly ritual. Unlike my daughter, my son did not get a story

about the fictitious kingdom of "Brumfield-Dom."
Instead, we would wrestle.

Night after night, I would grab my son in a
headlock and he would do the same to me. After that, I
would say, "I love this guy!" And then he would say, "I
love this man!" We would repeat the chokehold and the
phrases about three or four times, increasing our intensity
with each proclamation of our devotion. When we
concluded our nightly ritual, my son would fall asleep.
Maybe, the lack of oxygen from the chokehold put him
down—just kidding.

Whenever I share the story of my nightly ritual
with my children with people, I am commended for the
way I loved my children. I am applauded for providing
each child with a unique experience that catered to their
gender. But, according to Jesus, my care, my tenderness
and my concern for my children is inferior to God's care,
tenderness and concern for his children. God is more
hands on; God is more nurturing than you or I could ever
be.

God wants us to feel like my son felt as we
wrestled and declared our devotion; he felt a deep-bound

connection with me. God wants us to feel like my daughter felt as we escaped into our mythical kingdom; she felt love and security. As it was with my children, God wants to put you in his loving chokehold.

Yes, God wants you to know the Bible stories that convey his nature. Yes, the scriptures are the primary way that God reveals himself. However, as I did with my daughter, God wants to convey his love through personal stories, as well.

Unlike the stories that I created to bond with my daughter in the mythical kingdom of Brumfield-Dom, God wants to comfort you and me in the real world. In the trenches of life, where we strive to make a living, where the deck is often stacked against us, God wants to reveal himself to us as father and friend. He truly wants you and me to know that we are favored sons and daughters.

When we know that God has set his affection on us and is with us, we are sufficiently armed for the precarious and erratic nature of employment in today's economy. I'm not speaking from an ivory tower. My claim is birthed out of experience, both past and present.

After I finished writing the previous chapter, I had an unsettling feeling. I wondered whether this book would truly help people who are unemployed. Would the stories that I shared fuel faith in the face of employment uncertainty or would it appear that I was simply the beneficiary of some very timely luck. Moreover, I wanted some assurance that God endorsed my effort to write a book about my journey in corporate America.

With these two thoughts on my mind, while sipping my morning coffee at my kitchen table, I opened a letter marked *Urgent Timely Response*. The letter contained information from my medical provider. It appeared that my medical coverage was terminated. The European-based company that employed me decided to restructure their global IT operations. Consequently, I was the casualty of a corporate downsize.

How ironic to suddenly become unemployed while writing the final chapter of a book that encourages people who are unemployed. Generally, a layoff doesn't trigger laughter, but after I read the letter, I laughed. I felt that my twist of fate, due to the layoff, was God's way of saying, "Darryl, I'm with you. I want you to share your journey." After 12 years of service, my employment came to an abrupt end. Now, like many of the people that I hope will read this book, I was unemployed.

Besides my unexpected loss of income, I had a host of other pressing issues to contend with. My son was recently admitted into the emergency room for chest pains; we were praying together daily for a resolution. My wife, who had undergone two major surgeries in the past 24 months, was awaiting the results of a biopsy. The tenant in our rental home gave notice that she was moving, and before we could fill the vacancy, we needed to make some costly repairs to the property. Finally, because a building was leased in my name without my knowledge, in the previous week I received notice that a $28,000 judgment was entered against me. My counsel advised that the judgment could be overturned, but attorneys don't work for free. Life doesn't come to a screeching halt when your employment is terminated.

In many ways, my response to the layoff was typical. Like most people, I took a look at my war chest and calculated my burn rate. Fortunately, God had provided some reserves, but when your outflow is larger than your income, no matter how large your war chest may be, it never seems to be large enough. So whenever I felt anxiety, I would find refuge in the knowledge that I was a favored son.

I have learned through the years that sometimes you will face a perfect storm. No matter how many self-help books you buy, no matter what life principles you adopt, you and I will experience the inconvenient consequences of living in a broken world that is inhabited by broken people.

Still, at times it may seem like chaos reigns. Though we may be tempted to cast God as an absentee landlord or a disinterested father, I have learned that God is intimately engaged in the affairs of his children and he is in control of everything. God always has a plan and he is always working out his plan with orderly precision, even if our circumstances persuade us to think otherwise.

This final chapter does not contain the words that I initially wanted to write. In my mind, before I could share my stories, I needed to end my book, in material terms, on a high note. After all, getting laid off isn't quite the Hollywood ending that we have come to expect from an encouraging inspirational book.

Because I was on the verge of launching a successful internet company, I delayed writing the final chapter for almost a year. I was certain that the launch of my company would provide the big finish that I coveted. But my plan was not God's plan.

I may launch a successful internet company someday; it is not beyond my reach. Certainly, God is not opposed to my participation in a venture that results in great wealth. However, this book isn't about how to find the pot of gold at the end of the Technology rainbow. This book is about learning to think and live like a favored child. Knowing that you are the apple of God's eye is a wonderful feeling, but that fact doesn't guarantee that you will live happily ever after.

Too often, a book filled with one victorious testimony after another paints a rosy picture that misleads its reader in regards to trials. The truth is, you are either in a trial, exiting a trial or you are being prepared for a trial. I didn't write this book to encourage people to look for the light at the end of the tunnel. I wrote this book to empower people who are in the tunnel.

We all need encouragement, but empowerment is a superior virtue. When we are encouraged, we simply feel better about where we are. But when we are empowered, we move, we act, and we respond to our situation with the tools that God has given us.

I'm a storyteller and I love to use stories to empower people. My current crisis didn't change that. Consequently, I'm not waiting to see the light at the end of the tunnel before I do what I was put on this earth to do. I can move forward because I know that God will do what God always does. God will work out my situation according to his plan, and I will be the better for it.

Still, when you're out of work and you need to put some food on the table, it can seem like there is nothing bigger than a job. When it seems like your student loan has made you an indentured servant, a job that is both lucrative and fulfilling can consume your every thought. When rumors of layoffs and plant shutdowns are circulating through the corridors of your work place, fear and anxiety can become an obsession.

But, if we're honest, why does the precarious and competitive nature of our livelihood trouble us? Why do we feel so helpless? Why are we afraid? Better yet, what is the cure for our alarm?

I can say with certainty that the cure for employment anxiety is not finding a job; the cure is finding God. A healthy and accurate understanding of God's character is priceless. And to experience his character in the context of a relationship is better still.

How we see God determines how we see circumstances. It saddens me that so many people have a warped concept of God. Some see God, the creator of the universe, as their personal Genie. Some see God as a disconnected deity, one who only interacts with his creatures to reward those who obey him and to punish those who don't.

But God isn't Santa Clause; he is not checking his list twice to see who is naughty or nice. Neither is he standing at attention, waiting for his creatures to give him a command. Those views of God are twisted; they are not in agreement with the God of scripture.

The scriptures present a God that, while fully engaged in the lives of his creation, is not the servant of his creation. And, though God rewards obedience, God's merit system is not as simplistic as many Christians make it out to be.

I can cite countless examples in scripture where God blessed the naughty and allowed the nice to experience hardship. Yet, God is not fickle; God is fair and just. But most of all God is a perfect father to his children. All of these truths about God were not nullified because I was laid off.

We can never fully comprehend God in all his Glory, but God can be known. Jesus came to reveal God to men. Knowing our limitations, he used a human relationship to convey the character of a divine person.

The relationship of a father to his children is the relationship that Jesus used to reveal the character of God to men. At the end of the day, God wants us to understand the dynamics of that relationship. It's safe to say that everything we do on this earth is designed to lead us into a greater revelation of God, the Father. But what kind of father is God?

Jesus used parables to correct our thinking about God. His parables would depict a God who actually liked his children. Although I was raised in a Christian home, I didn't know that God liked me. Oh, I knew that God loved me. From a child I was taught that God sent Jesus to die in my place. I was taught that this supreme sacrifice proved that God loved me; after all, he paid my sin invoice. But does the story end there?

God is more than a father who pays the bills. We all know fathers who love their families, and yet they don't really like their families. Yes, they pay the mortgage on time, put food on the table and pay school tuition. They do all of these things because they love their families, but they really do not like their families. Given a choice, they prefer the golf course to the home.

But God not only loves his children, God likes his children. That's what the parables about Father God convey. God is more than a provider; he is engaged, he is tender and caring; he likes us. He is the type of father that doesn't miss a single Little League at bat or one note of a recital.

God's children are a priority not an afterthought. God is a can't-wait-to-get-home, help-you-with-your-homework type of dad; God is engaged with his children. At the end of the day, this book contains some of my favorite life-changing homework assignments.

But when you are worried about your next paycheck or whether your unemployment dollars will meet your needs, it's easy to forget that God is a loving father. I (you) have been there, and when I started writing this chapter I was there again. But I find comfort in this fact: God's love for me surpasses the love I have for my children.

I have been unemployed and under-employed. I have lost more jobs than I have found, but more jobs have found me than I can count, that's the story that I wanted to tell. For in telling that story, the heart of Father God was revealed to me. He used my career as his canvas.

God has taken his brush and painted a beautiful picture—a picture of a loving father, a father who is always several steps ahead of his son, using my mistakes not to just scold me but mold me. And in the process, he showed me that he was behind the scenes orchestrating the events that provided the many teaching moments that I shared.

God wants all of his children to experience the love that John experienced, the love that my children experienced and the love that he has extended to me. God wants all of us to have a deep bond with him, deeper than any other relationship that you may have experienced. He used my IT career to help me experience this deep bond. This deep bond is priceless; its riches can't be measured. You can have church, religion and knowledge of scripture and not have a relationship with God that has depth.

A deep relationship with God occurs when God is no longer abstract. To have a deep relationship with God, God must become a real person. God must become someone that you talk to and share life with. John stated it this way, "This is Eternal Life to know God the father and Jesus who he sent."

Can you say that you know God? Have you ever just sat down with him and shared your most intimate thoughts and fears? Is God your friend? If so, when was the last time you laughed so hard that your side ached as you spent time with him?

As you look over your life are you in awe of both God's favor towards you and his complete control over your circumstances? Can you understand the sentiments expressed by David, as he calls God "Sovereign Lord"[35] and declares the there is no one like him? If so, you are beginning to understand what it means to be a favorite son or daughter. If not, I invite you to ask God to reveal himself to you.

When we ask God to reveal himself, we discover that God, without an invitation, was already working in our life though we were not aware it. God is always the initiator. He is the master orchestrator. He is the architect of our past, present and our future. That's a pretty scary thought if we don't know God's character. But if we, through the circumstances of life and the truth of his word, really come to know God then the

[35] 2 Samuel 7:18-22

understanding that God is in control isn't scary. It's empowering.

In closing, to date, my career in technology has not yielded a financial windfall but, I don't feel the least bit slighted. My contentment, in part, is rooted in my intimate relationship with God, a relationship that he developed through trials and tests, while I was employed, under-employed, and unemployed. Through it all, I have learned some priceless truths. Chiefly, I am not an orphan; like the apostle John, I am the favored child that God loves. But if you are God's child then you are a favored child of God too, and that means that like David, you don't have to fear your giants. Instead, you can listen to God and slay them.